ALL-IN-ONE PIANO COURSE
Lessons • Technique • Theory • Online Support

ADULT PIANO

2

PIANO
Adventures® *by Nancy and Randall Faber*

Production Coordinator: Jon Ophoff
Cover: Terpstra Design, San Francisco
Engraving: Dovetree Productions, Inc.

FABER
PIANO ADVENTURES®

Book Only ISBN 978-1-61677-334-2
Book & Disc Set ISBN 978-1-61677-332-8

Welcome

Continuing from Book 1?

This sequel continues your musical journey at the keyboard. Over two hours of instructional video provide a professional perspective to accelerate your musical training. Supporting audio tracks convey a sonic world of rhythm, melody, and harmony.

Enhance your learning with instructional videos by world-renowned pianist and educator Randall Faber.

Returning to the Piano?

If you had piano lessons previously, this is your opportunity to gain confidence at the keyboard. Learn to read and play lead sheets, polish your technique and increase your overall musical understanding. Take time to find and develop the expressive dimension in your playing.

Energize your Brain!

New and familiar melodies, basic music theory, creative exploration, and musical expressivity provide stimulation and enrichment!

How This Book is Organized

You will study 16 units, each covering a new concept while providing review of previous topics and skills.

Concepts are displayed in a shaded file folder.

Practice suggestions guide your first steps.

Discovery questions invite deeper analysis and creative activities engage your brain in new ways.

Online video and audio tracks are noted at the bottom of corresponding pages. When you see these icons, visit pianoadventures.com/adult

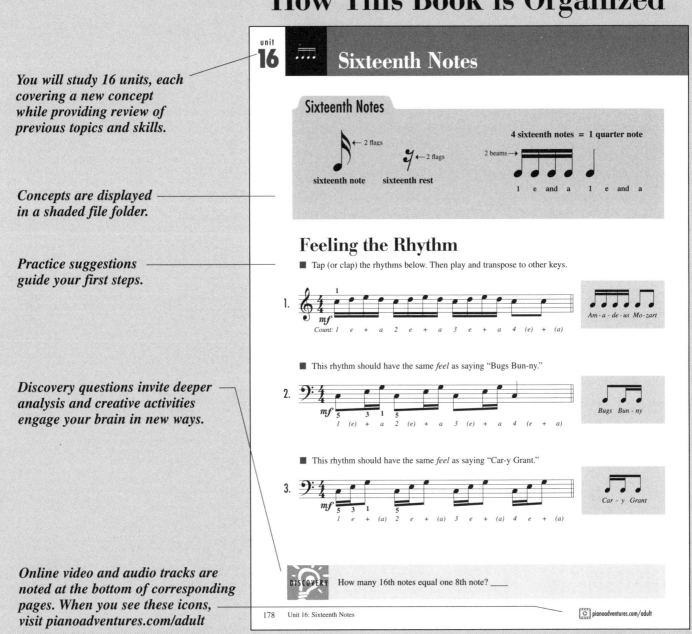

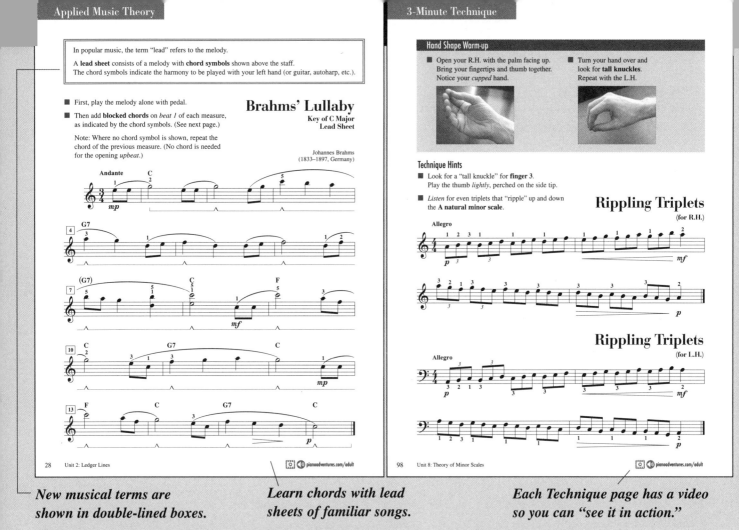

New musical terms are shown in double-lined boxes.

Learn chords with lead sheets of familiar songs.

Each Technique page has a video so you can "see it in action."

At the end of each unit, you will find 3-Minute Technique and Applied Music Theory pages. Technique pages develop an optimal physical approach to the piano, and build finger dexterity in just three minutes a day. Applied Music Theory pages help you learn chords and harmony while increasing your reading skills.

Enhanced Audio Support

Download the Piano Adventures Player™ app for interactive accompaniment tracks that adjust to any tempo. Fun and easy to use!

Expand your repertoire!

Play dozens of familiar songs at just the right level in the Adult Piano Adventures supplementary books. Choose among your favorite genres, including Popular, Classics, and Christmas.

Contents

5

Music Fundamentals (Review of Book 1)

Note Values

Note values and their rests indicate the duration of sound.
These durations are counted with a steady beat, creating RHYTHM.

■ Draw each note or rest in the boxes provided.

Notes			Rests		
whole note 4 beats "1-2-3-4"	𝅝		**whole rest** silence for any *whole* measure	▬	
			Note: This would apply for $\frac{4}{4}$, $\frac{3}{4}$, $\frac{2}{4}$, or any other time signature.		
dotted half note 3 beats "1-2-3"	𝅗𝅥.				
half note 2 beats "1-2"	𝅗𝅥		**half rest** 2 beats of silence	▬	
quarter note 1 beat "1"	♩		**quarter rest** 1 beat of silence	𝄽	
eighth note 1/2 beat	♪		**eighth rest** 1/2 beat of silence (presented on p. 64)	𝄾	
two eighth notes = 1 quarter note "1 and"	♫ and				

pianoadventures.com/adult

Time Signatures

The two numbers written at the beginning of a piece of music show the **time signature**.

Ex. **3**—The *top* number indicates the number of beats per measure.
4—The *bottom* number represents the kind of note receiving one beat.
The 4 = quarter = ♩

1. Tap (or clap) this ²₄ rhythm, counting aloud. Then choose any key and play, using finger 3. (+ = "and")

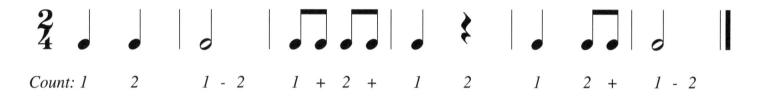

Count: 1   2   1 - 2   1 + 2 +   1   2   1   2 +   1 - 2

2. Tap (or clap) this ³₄ rhythm, counting aloud. Then choose any key and play, using finger 3.

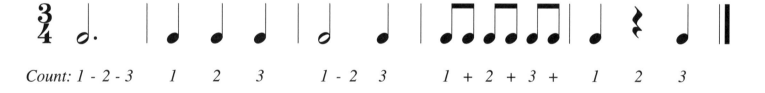

Count: 1 - 2 - 3   1   2   3   1 - 2   3   1 + 2 + 3 +   1   2   3

3. Tap (or clap) this ⁴₄ rhythm, counting aloud. Then choose any key and play, using finger 3.

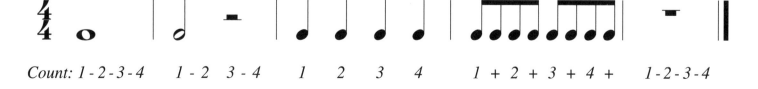

Count: 1 - 2 - 3 - 4   1 - 2   3 - 4   1   2   3   4   1 + 2 + 3 + 4 +   1 - 2 - 3 - 4

Bass Clef and Treble Clef

Bass refers to *low* sounds.

The two dots of the **bass clef** point out the **F line**.

F line — 𝄢

For this reason, the bass clef is also known as the **F clef**.

Treble refers to *high* sounds.

The **treble clef** circles around the **G line**.

G line —

For this reason, the treble clef is also known as the **G clef**.

Notes on the Grand Staff

Piano music uses two 5-line staves (staffs), connected by a brace and a bar line. Together they form the GRAND STAFF.

■ Play these notes on the keyboard from *lowest* to *highest*, saying the note names aloud. Use left hand (L.H.) for bass clef notes; right hand (R.H.) for treble clef notes.

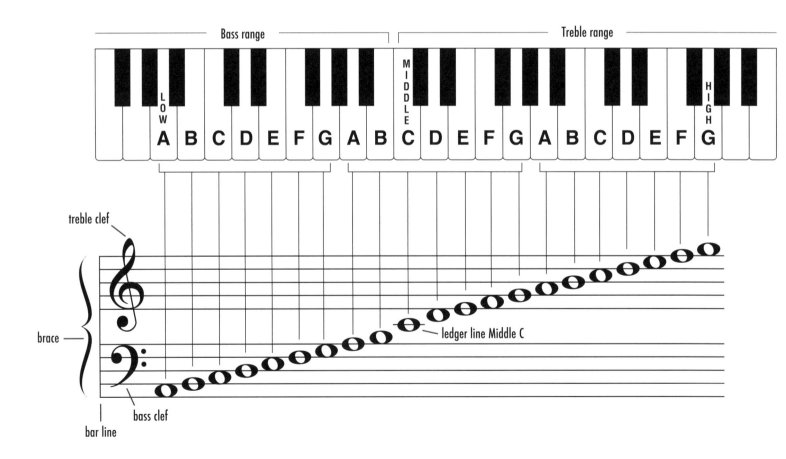

Dynamic Marks

The word **dynamics** comes from the Greek word for "power."
In music, *dynamics* means the "louds and softs" of the sound.

■ Choose any key on the piano and play it at each of these dynamic marks.
Listen to the change in sound.

Symbol	Term	Definition	Pronunciation
pp	*pianissimo*	very soft	"pyah-NEES-see-moh"
p	*piano*	soft	"PYAH-noh"
mp	*mezzo piano*	moderately soft	"MET-tsoh PYAH-noh"
mf	*mezzo forte*	moderately loud	"MET-tsoh FOR-tay"
f	*forte*	loud	"FOR-tay"
ff	*fortissimo*	very loud	"for-TEES-see-moh"

crescendo (cresc.)   *diminuendo (dim.)*
                                  or *decrescendo (decresc.)*

Play gradually louder.   Play gradually softer.

■ Play, observing the dynamic marks.

Dynamic Study

Depress the damper (right foot) pedal.   *Lift.*

Intervals

An **interval** is the distance between two musical *tones*, *keys* on the keyboard, or *notes* on the staff.

■ Play the examples on these pages. Notice that each interval is played two ways:

    broken—the notes are played *melodically* (separately)

    blocked—the notes are played *harmonically* (together)

Second (2nd)

A 2nd spans adjacent letter names (Ex. C–D). On the staff, the interval of a 2nd is from:

a LINE to the next SPACE   or   **a SPACE to the next LINE**

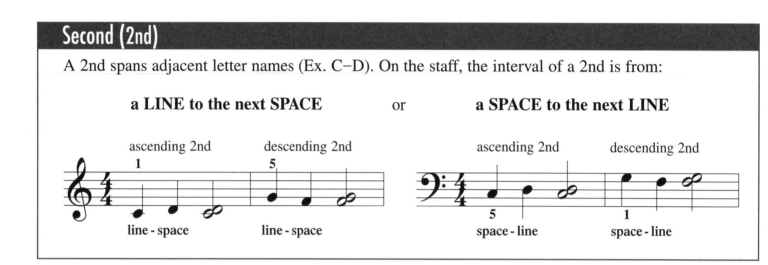

Third (3rd)

A 3rd skips a letter name (Ex. C–E). On the staff, the interval of a 3rd is from:

a LINE to the next LINE   or   **a SPACE to the next SPACE**

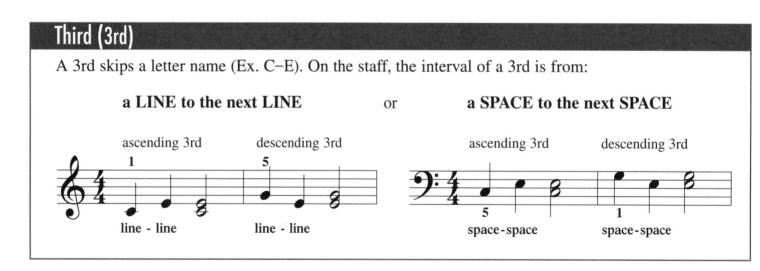

Fourth (4th)

A 4th spans four letter names (Ex. C–F). On the staff, the interval of a 4th is from:

a LINE *(skip-a-line)* **to a SPACE**   or   **a SPACE** *(skip-a-space)* **to a LINE**

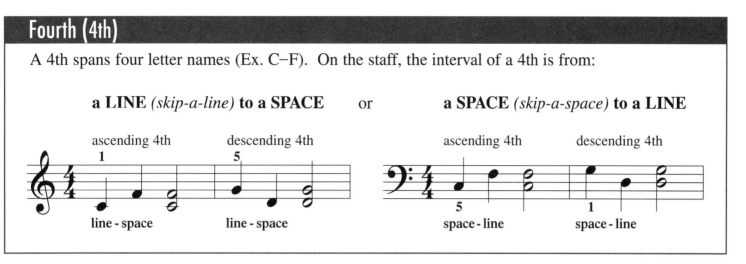

Fifth (5th)

A 5th spans five letter names (Ex. C–G). On the staff, the interval of a 5th is from:

a LINE *(skip-a-line)* **to a LINE**   or   **a SPACE** *(skip-a-space)* **to a SPACE**

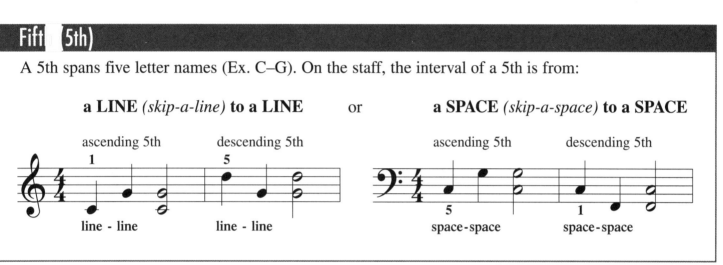

Sixth (6th)

A 6th spans six letter names (Ex. E–C). On the staff, the interval of a 6th is from:

a LINE *(skip 2 lines)* **to a SPACE**   or   **a SPACE** *(skip 2 spaces)* **to a LINE**

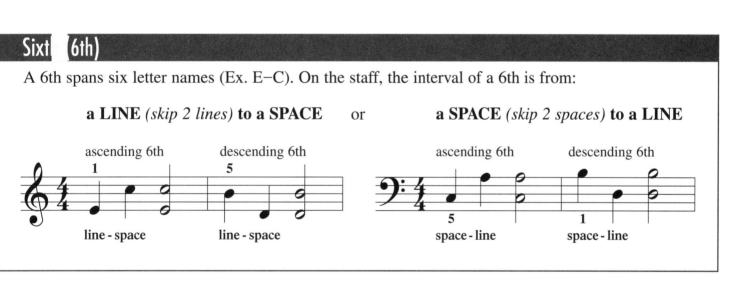

Reading Hints

The *odd-numbered* intervals (3rd, 5th) are always **line to line** or **space to space**.

The *even-numbered* intervals (2nd, 4th, 6th) are always **line to space** or **space to line**.

Key of C Major

The C Major Scale

A **major scale** is made of **whole steps** except for half steps between *scale degrees 3–4* and *7–8*.
See the Dictionary of Musical Terms on p. 196 for review of whole steps (W) and half steps (H).

■ Play the C major scale below hands alone, then hands together.

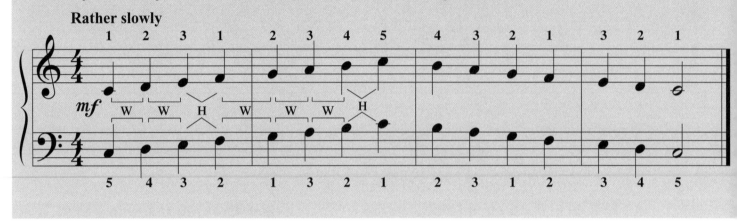

Primary Chords in C Major: I-IV-V

Chords can be built in **3rds** on each *degree* of the scale (scale step).
The **primary chords** (**I**, **IV**, and **V** or **V7**) are built on *scale degrees 1, 4,* and *5* of the scale.

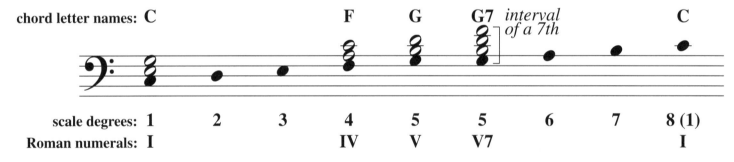

■ With your L.H., play the I, IV, V, and V7 chords shown above.
These chords are in ROOT POSITION: the letter name of the chord *(the root)* is the lowest tone.

C Major: Primary Chords in Close Position

Chord tones can be *inverted* (rearranged) to eliminate keyboard leaps.

■ With your L.H., play the close position I, IV, and V7 chords shown below.
The roots of the chords are shaded.

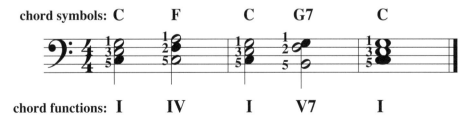

(How the chord is *functioning* in a given key. For example, the F chord functions as the IV chord in the Key of C.)

Key of G Major

The G Major Scale

■ Play the G major scale below hands alone, then hands together.

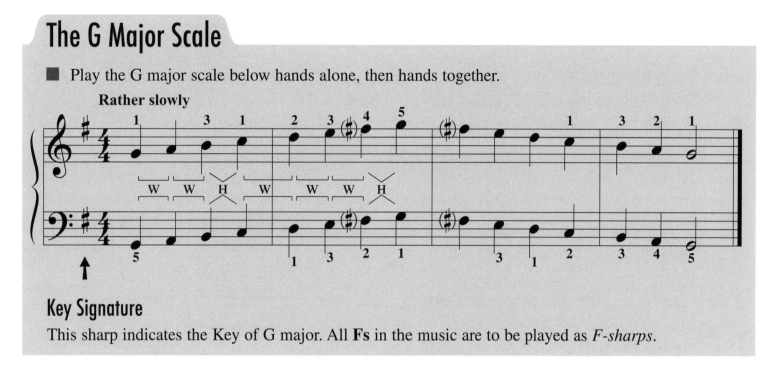

Key Signature

This sharp indicates the Key of G major. All **Fs** in the music are to be played as *F-sharps*.

Primary Chords in G Major: I-IV-V

The **primary chords** for the Key of G major are shown below in ROOT POSITION.

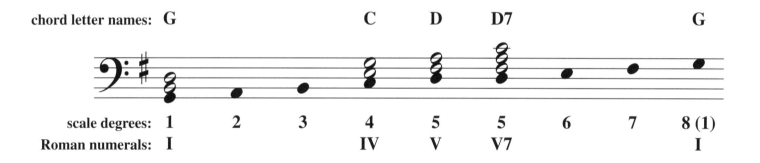

■ With your L.H., play the I, IV, V, and V7 chords shown above.

G Major: Primary Chords in Close Position

■ With your L.H., play the close position I, IV, and V7 chords shown below.

Musical Form

Musical form is the overall structure of a piece.

Binary Form or A B Form

"Binary" means two parts. Two-part form has an **A** section followed by a **B** section. In binary form, each section usually has a repeat sign.

‖: **A** :‖: **B** :‖

■ Point out these sections in the music below.

Allegro Moderato
Review Piece

Nancy Faber

A SECTION

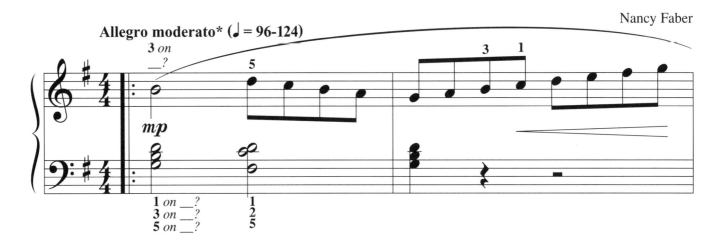

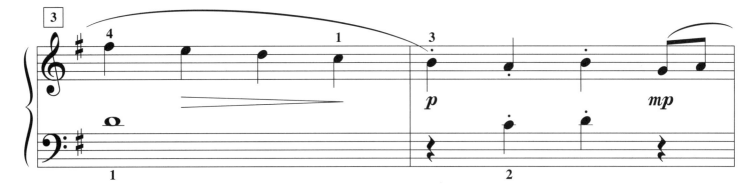

Teacher Duet: (Student plays *1 octave higher*)

Allegro moderato–moderately fast

🔊 pianoadventures.com/adult

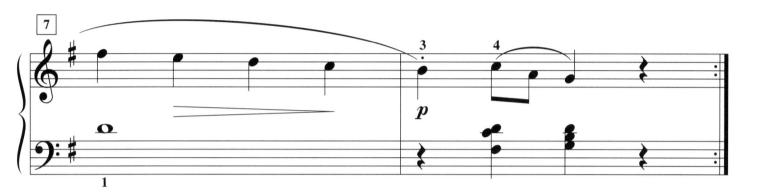

B SECTION

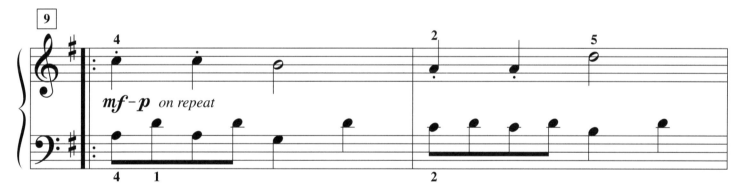

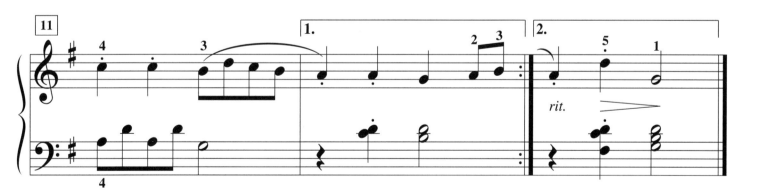

Review: **Transposition** means playing the same music in a different key.
The note names change, but the *intervals* stay the same.
Transpose *Allegro Moderato* to the **Key of C Major**.

Ledger Lines

A **ledger line** is a short line added above or below the staff for notes that are too high or too low to be written on the staff.

LOW C is located 2 ledger lines *below* the bass clef staff.
HIGH C is located 2 ledger lines *above* the treble clef staff.

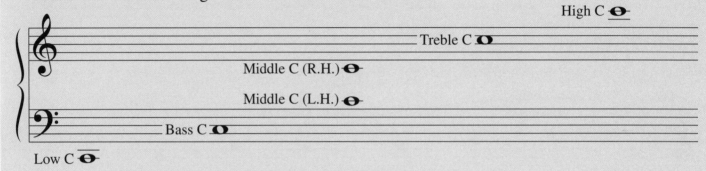

- Play each C shown above, saying its correct name.
  Review: From one C to the next C is the interval of an *octave* (8 notes).

Technique Hint

- *Measures 1–4:* Play with an open hand and extended fingers to comfortably play the octaves.

Octave Warm-up

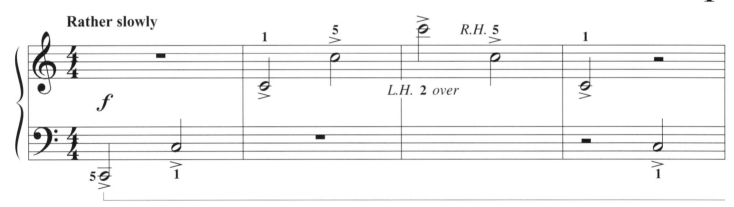

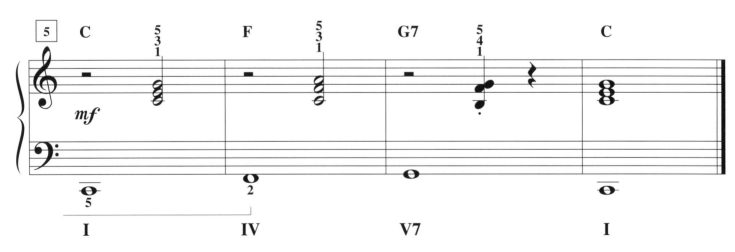

 DISCOVERY Transpose *Octave Warm-up* to the **Key of G Major.**

pianoadventures.com/adult

Cathedral Chimes

Quickly, joyously

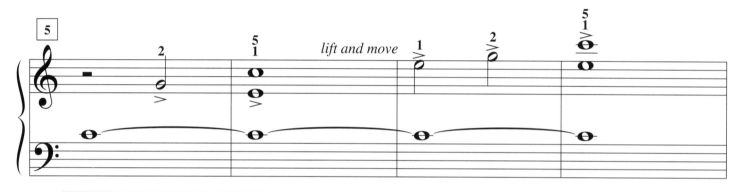

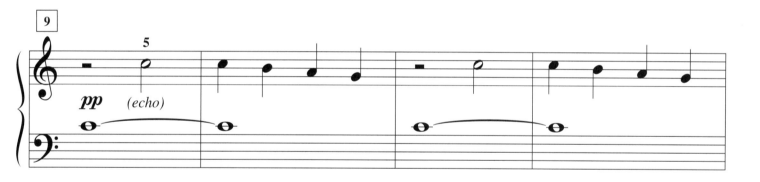

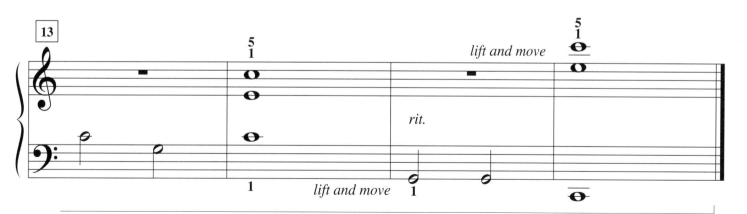

 DISCOVERY   Which two lines of music use only notes of the **C major chord**?

D.C. al Coda

Da Capo al Coda means "from the top to the *Coda*."
Return to the beginning and play to ⊕, then jump to
the *Coda* (ending).

Niagara Falls
Key of C Major

Nancy Faber

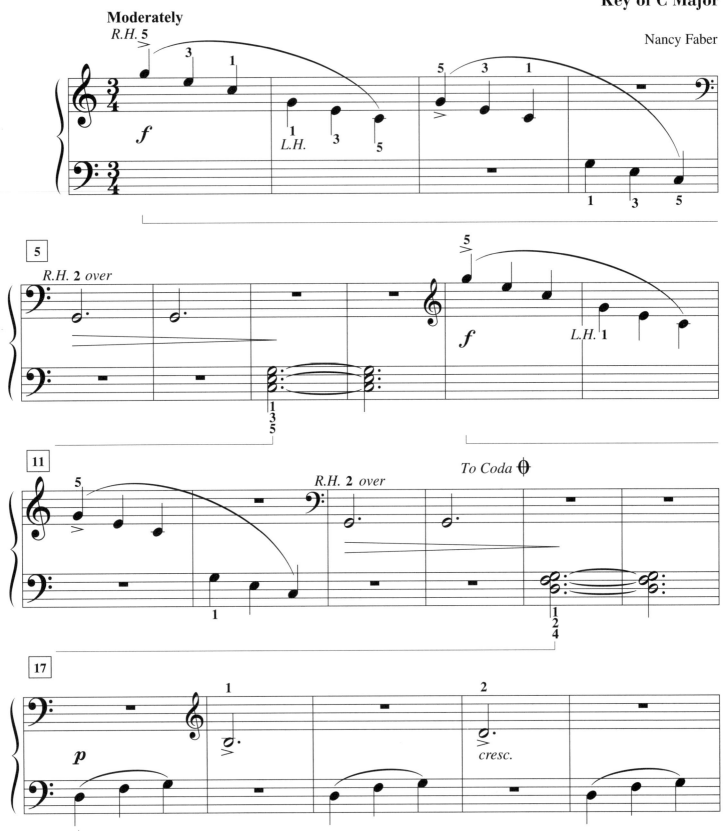

pianoadventures.com/adult

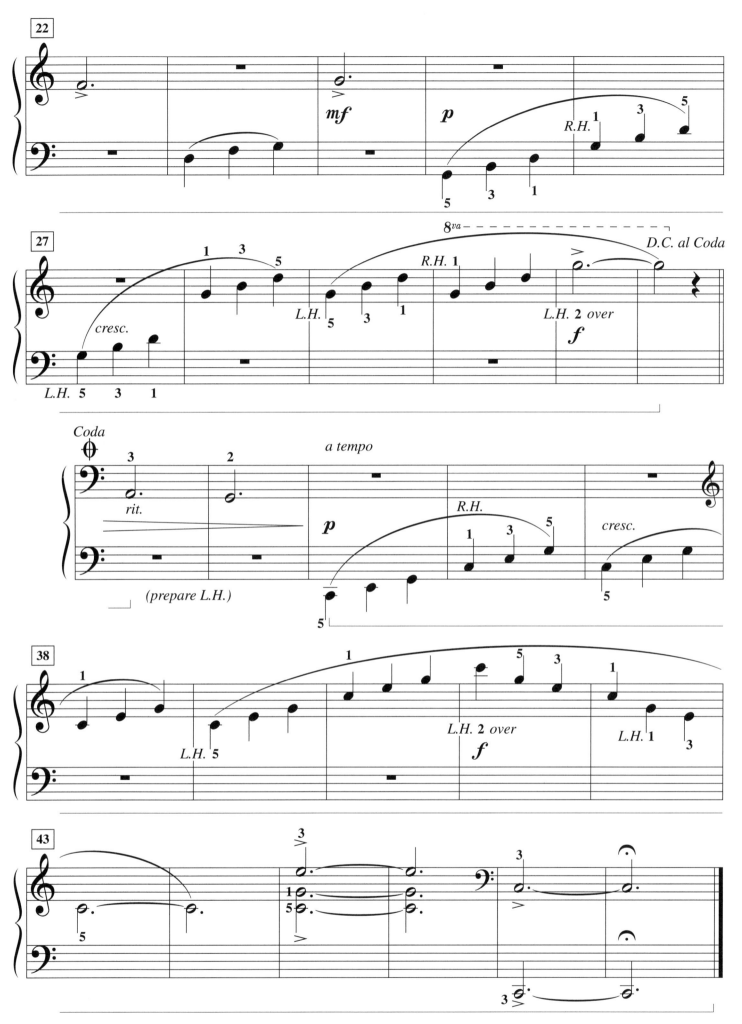

DISCOVERY Find 8 consecutive measures that use only notes of the **G major chord**.

Connected Pedaling

Connected pedaling will make the music sound *legato* (connected).

1. Say these words aloud as you practice this foot motion.

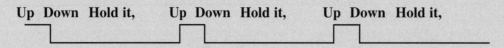

Up Down Hold it,   Up Down Hold it,   Up Down Hold it,

2. The pedal mark ‿ indicates exactly the same foot motion practiced above.
    Lift the damper pedal on the beat, then depress it again after the keys are played.

(Up) Down Hold it,   Up Down Hold it,   Up Down Hold it,

Pedal Hints

■ Say the words aloud as you play. Notice that the pedal is depressed AFTER the chord is struck.

■ Prepare the next chord during *beats 3* and *4*.

■ *Listen* carefully for a smooth, connected sound.

Pedal Exercise

Moderately

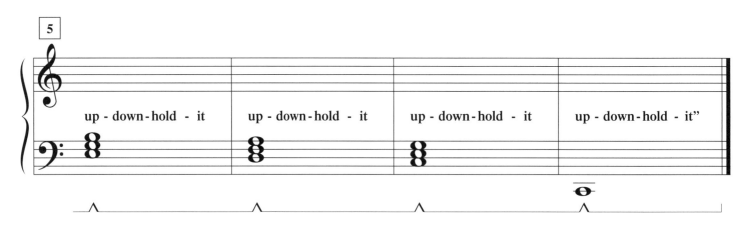

mp
Say: "Up-down-hold - it   up-down-hold - it   up-down-hold - it   up-down-hold - it
Beats: 1 - 2 - 3 - 4

(move hand)   (move hand)

5

up-down-hold - it   up-down-hold - it   up-down-hold - it   up-down-hold - it"

DISCOVERY Play *Pedal Exercise* **hands together**.
(R.H. plays the same chord 1 octave *higher*.)

20   Unit 2: Ledger Lines

The bugle call *Taps* as we know it today had its origins on a battlefield of the Civil War. After the Union suffered extensive casualties in a battle near Richmond, Virginia, Colonel Daniel Butterfield reflected with sadness upon the men he had lost. Reportedly, he hummed a melody that his aide transcribed. The company bugler played it that night to signal "lights out," and other brigades quickly adopted it. Officially recognized by the United States Army in 1874, it is performed to this day whenever a service member is buried with military honors.

Practice Suggestions

- First practice *without* pedal, concentrating on the L.H. position changes.

- Then play *with* pedal. Observe all the **dynamic marks** for an expressive sound.

Taps
(for L.H. alone)

Traditional

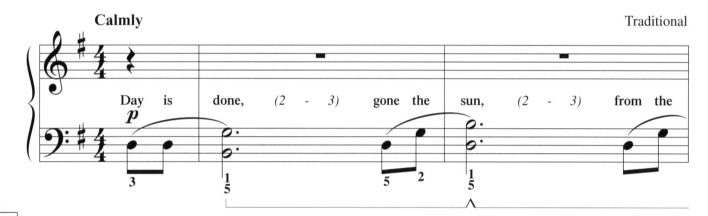

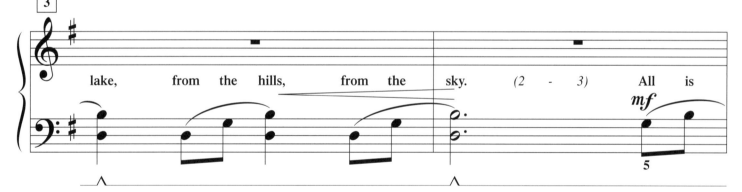

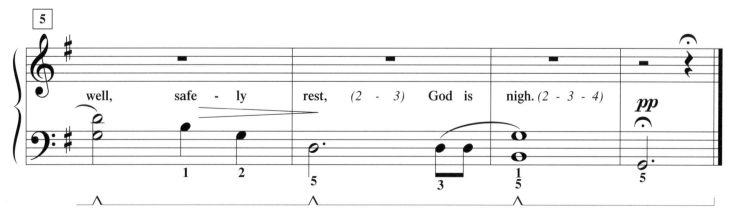

 DISCOVERY On which beat does this piece begin?

New Ledger Line Notes

■ Play these notes on the keyboard.

C   B   A

Alternate V7 Chord in Close Position

Instead of B, D can be the lowest note of a 3-note V7 chord.
(The full, 4-note V7 includes G-B-D-F.)

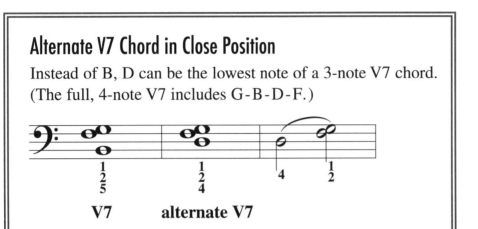

V7   alternate V7

'O Sole Mio!

Key of ____ Major

Eduardo di Capua
(1864–1917, Italy)
arranged

*Andante—walking speed

pianoadventures.com/adult

The form of this piece is section **A** followed by section **A¹**.
Mark the sections in the music. What is different about section **A¹**?

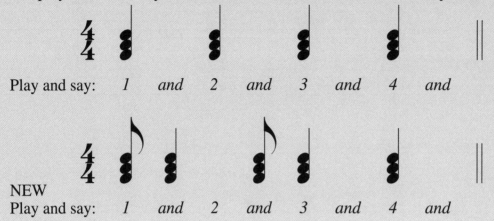

- Tap and count aloud.
  Each beat is divided into two parts: **1 and**, **2 and**, **3 and**, **4 and**.

- Now play these two rhythms on a **I**, **IV**, then **V7** chord in the **Key of G**.

Play and say: *1   and   2   and   3   and   4   and*

NEW
Play and say: *1   and   2   and   3   and   4   and*

Yellow Bird

Key of ____ Major

West Indies Folk Song
arranged

Cheerfully (♩ = 104)

pianoadventures.com/adult

 DISCOVERY Transpose *Yellow Bird* to the **Key of C Major**.

Pedal Hints

- Always keep your heel on the floor.

- The UP motion of the pedal occurs as the key is struck.
  The pedal goes DOWN immediately *after* the note is played.

- Use the half rests to prepare L.H. finger 3 over the next key.

Pedaling the Scale
(for L.H.)

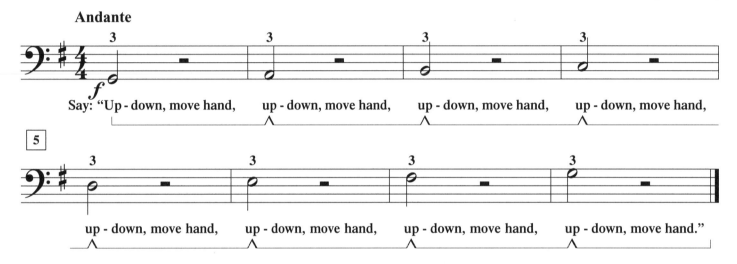

- Now repeat the exercise **hands together** (R.H. plays 2 *octaves higher*).

Pedaling Intervals
(for L.H.)

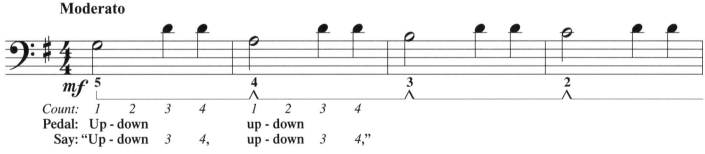

- Transpose *Pedaling Intervals* to the **Key of C Major**.

pianoadventures.com/adult

Technique Hints

■ Drop with arm weight into the **Low C** ledger notes.
Then lift from the wrist to prepare the upcoming chord.

■ Play the chords close to the keys, with wrists relaxed.

Pedaling Chords

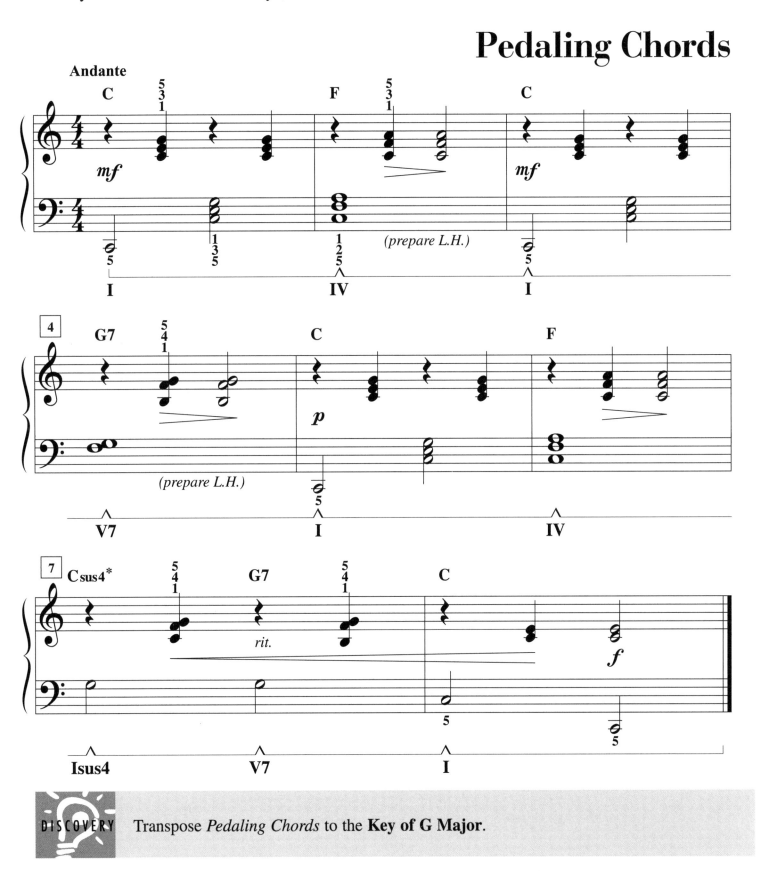

DISCOVERY   Transpose *Pedaling Chords* to the **Key of G Major**.

* **sus4** is the abbreviation for **suspended 4th.** The **Csus4 chord** uses a 4th above C (which is F)
instead of a 3rd above C (which is E). (See Book 1, p. 77.)

In popular music, the term "lead" refers to the melody.

A **lead sheet** consists of a melody with **chord symbols** shown above the staff.
The chord symbols indicate the harmony to be played with your left hand (or guitar, autoharp, etc.).

■ First, play the melody alone with pedal.

■ Then add **blocked chords** on *beat 1* of each measure, as indicated by the chord symbols. (See next page.)

Note: Where no chord symbol is shown, repeat the chord of the previous measure. (No chord is needed for the opening *upbeat*.)

Brahms' Lullaby

Key of C Major
Lead Sheet

Johannes Brahms
(1833–1897, Germany)

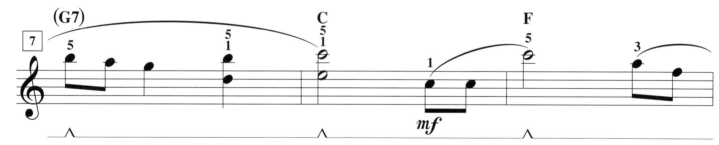

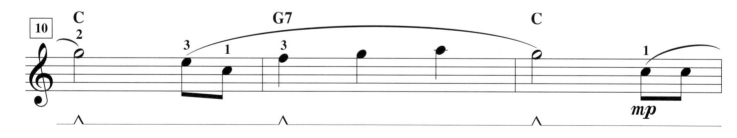

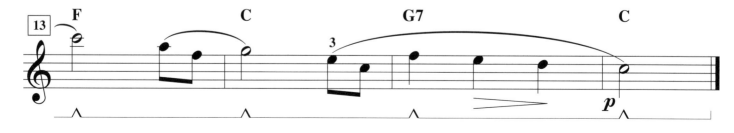

pianoadventures.com/adult

Chord References

Practice the chords used in *Brahms' Lullaby*. The **root** of each chord is circled.

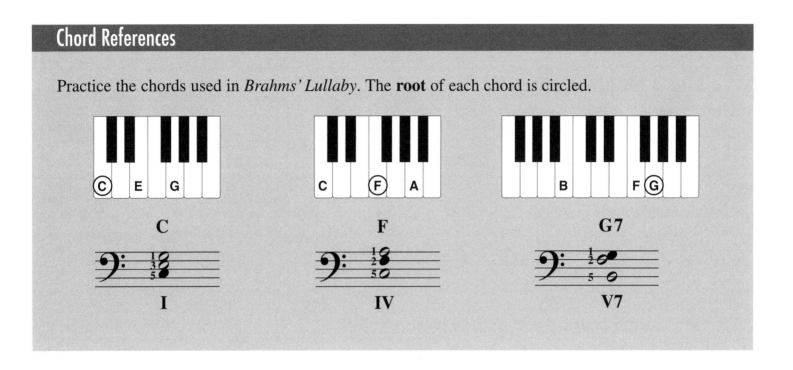

Broken-Chord Accompaniment

accompaniment—notes or chords that support the melody

When you can comfortably play *Brahms' Lullaby* with **blocked chords**, practice playing the melody with this L.H. accompaniment pattern.

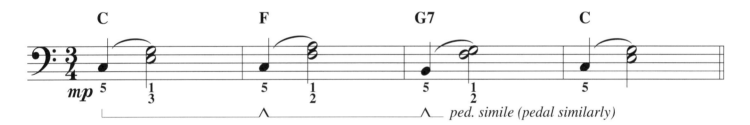

ped. simile (pedal similarly)

The F Major Scale

The F Major Scale

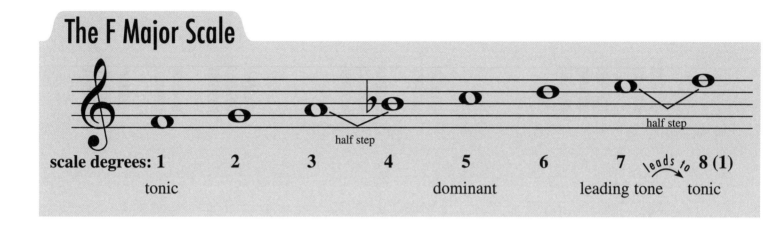

scale degrees: **1**   **2**   **3**   **4**   **5**   **6**   **7** *leads to* **8 (1)**

tonic   dominant   leading tone   tonic

half step

half step

Review: a **major scale** is made of **whole steps** except for
half steps between *scale degrees 3–4* and *7–8*.

Find and play these tones in the Key of F Major:

- ■ Scale degree 1,
  the **tonic (F)**.

- ■ Scale degree 5,
  the **dominant (C)**.

- ■ Scale degree 7,
  the **leading tone (E)**.
  It is a half step below F.

Listen and Discover

- ■ Using R.H. finger 3, play the F major scale and stop on the *leading tone*.
  Do you hear how the *leading tone* pulls up to the *tonic* note F?

- ■ Complete the scale by playing the tonic note.

Key Signature for F Major

The half step between *scale degrees 3–4* requires
the **B** (scale degree 4) to be flatted (**B♭**).

Since the F major scale has a B-flat, a piece in the
Key of F Major will use B-flats throughout.

Instead of a flat appearing before every B in the piece,
a flat is shown on the B line at the beginning of each
staff. This is called the **key signature**.

pianoadventures.com/adult

F Scale Warm-ups

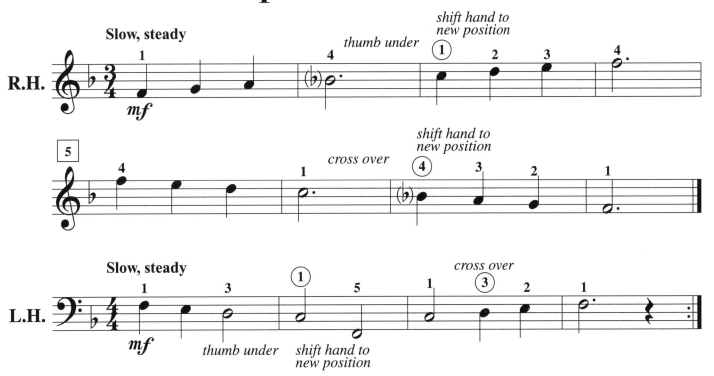

Playing the F Major Scale

■ Practice s-l-o-w-l-y, listening for an even tone.

■ Memorize the fingering for each hand.

The L.H. fingering for the F major scale is the same as the L.H. fingering for the C and G major scales.

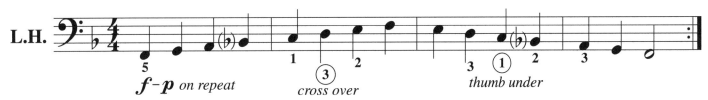

Metronome Practice

Put a ✓ in the blank when you can play the F major scale **hands alone** at these tempi.
Play each hand *ascending*, then *descending*.

legato ♩ = 88 ___	*legato* ♩ = 112 ___	*legato* ♩ = 144 ___
staccato ♩ = 88 ___	*staccato* ♩ = 112 ___	*staccato* ♩ = 144 ___

Phrase

A **phrase** is a musical idea, often indicated by a long slur called a *phrase mark*.

Phrase marks show where a singer might breathe. A pianist may "breathe with the wrist" by lifting gently at the end of each phrase.

Sloop John B

Key of ____ Major

Traditional

pianoadventures.com/adult

DISCOVERY Mark the **introduction** and **coda** in this piece.

Primary Chords in F Major: I - IV - V7

Review: The **I**, **IV**, and **V7** chords are built on *scale degrees 1, 4,* and *5* of the major scale.

■ Find and play the ROOT POSITION primary chords in the **Key of F**, shown below.

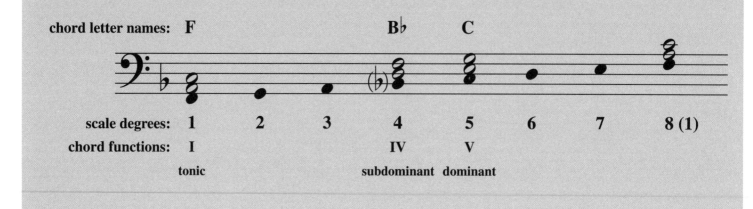

chord letter names:	F		Bb	C			

scale degrees:	1	2	3	4	5	6	7	8 (1)
chord functions:	I			IV	V			
	tonic			subdominant	dominant			

Inverting the IV Chord: Bb

To eliminate the leap between the **I** and **IV** chords (**F** chord to **Bb** chord),
the notes of the **IV** chord can be *inverted*.

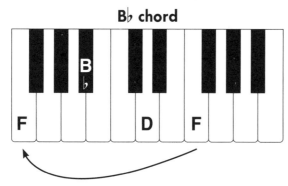

The F moves down an octave.

F Major: I-IV Chords in Close Position

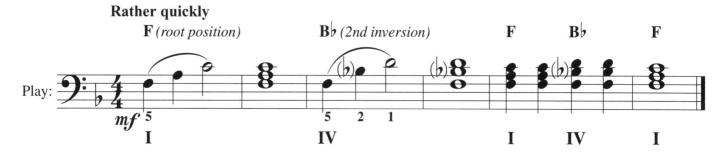

Draw pedal marks for the exercise above.
Hint: The pedal should change for each new harmony.

The V7 Chord in F Major: C7

A **7th chord** is a four-note chord built up in 3rds: The **C7** chord is **C - E - G - B♭**.

When the root (C) is the *lowest* note, the chord is in ROOT POSITION.

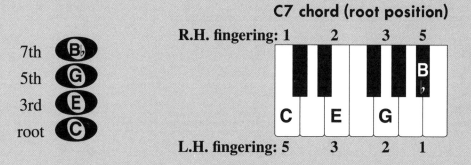

7th B♭
5th G
3rd E
root C

C7 chord (root position)

R.H. fingering: 1　2　3　5

L.H. fingering: 5　3　2　1

C is *scale degree 5* (the dominant) in the Key of F.

The **C7** chord is the **V7** or **dominant 7th** chord in the Key of F.

Inverting the V7 Chord: C7

To eliminate the leap between the **I** and **V7** chords (**F** chord to **C7** chord),
the notes of the **V7** chord are often inverted, with one of the chord tones omitted.

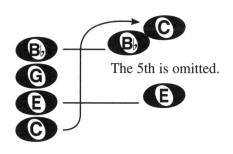

The 5th is omitted.

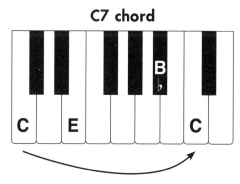

C7 chord

The C moves up an octave.

F Major: I-IV-V7 Chords in Close Position

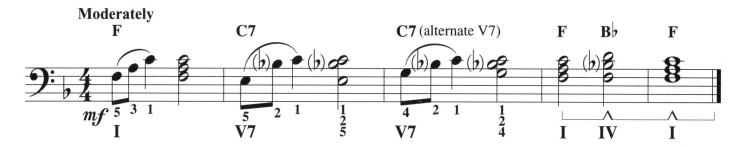

Motive

a short musical idea

Imitation

the immediate repetition of a musical idea in a different "voice" (in the other hand or in a different octave)

Allegro in F Major

Ferdinand Beyer
(1803-1863, Germany)
original form

■ In this piece, a R.H. motive is *imitated* by the L.H.

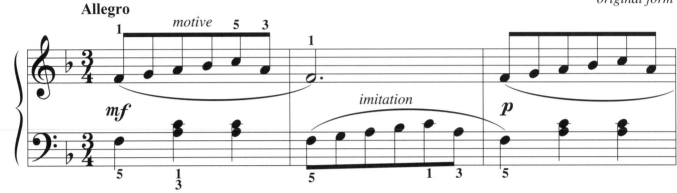

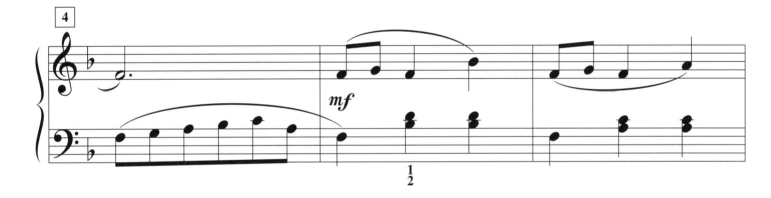

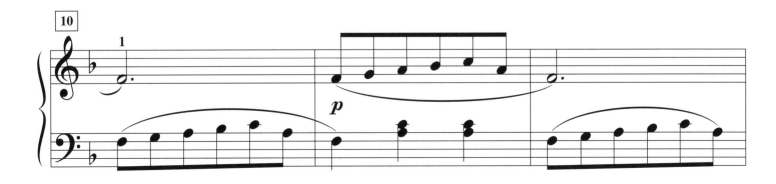

pianoadventures.com/adult

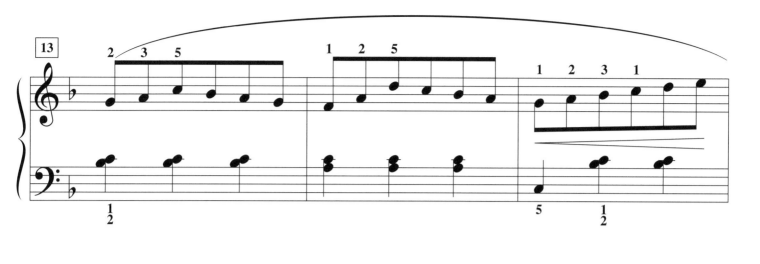

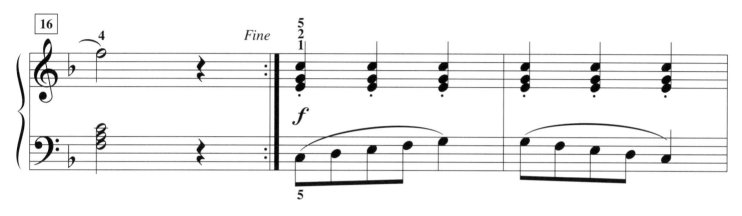

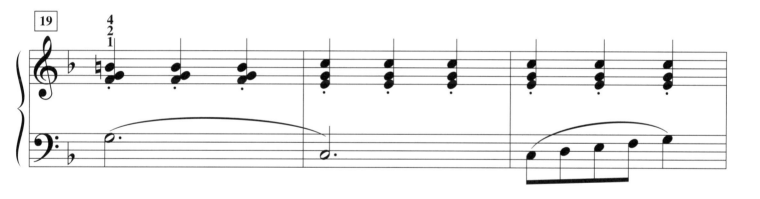

D.C. al Fine

 DISCOVERY   Write **I**, **IV**, or **V7** below the bass staff for *measures 1–16*.

Swing Rhythm

In many jazz and blues pieces, **8th notes** are played in a *long-short* pattern known as **swing rhythm**. Whenever the tempo mark includes the word "swing," play the 8th notes in swing rhythm.

■ Practice tapping the 8th notes below in "swing." (Teacher Note: ♫ = ♪³♪)

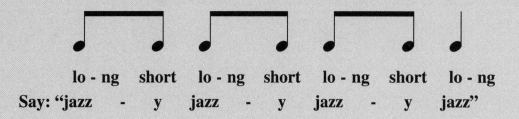

long   short   lo - ng   short   lo - ng   short   lo - ng
Say: "jazz   - y   jazz   - y   jazz   - y   jazz"

The Lion Sleeps Tonight

Words and Music by George David Weiss,
Hugo Peretti, Luigi Creatore, and Solomon Linda.

pianoadventures.com/adult

F Major Scale Hints

Both thumbs play on C.

- First practice s-l-o-w-l-y, concentrating on **fingering** and **dynamics**.

- Use firm fingertips for even 8th notes and control of each $<$ and $>$.

Scale Etude in F
(Op. 101)

Ferdinand Beyer
original form

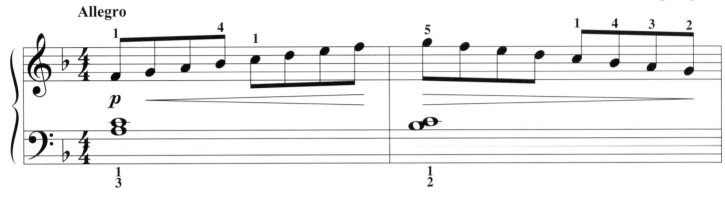

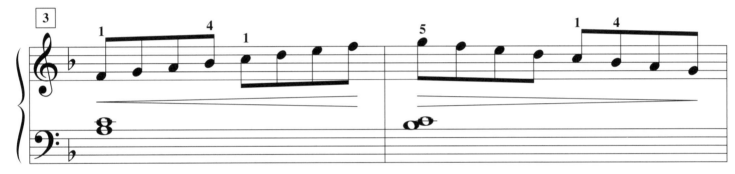

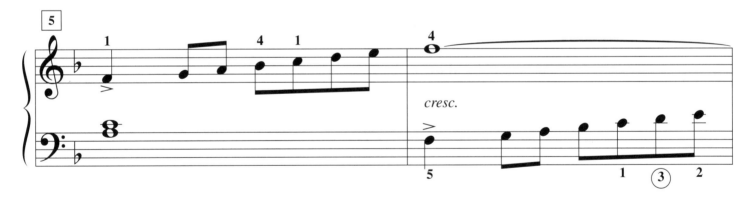

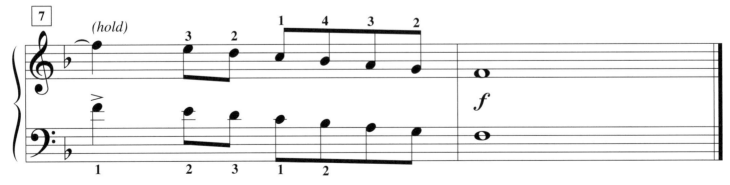

- Optional: Play *Scale Etude in F* using **swing rhythm.**

pianoadventures.com/adult

Rotation

With your R.H., make the motion of turning a key in a lock.
At the piano, this back-and-forth rocking motion is called **rotation**.

■ Practice the R.H. alone using **rotation**.

■ Then play hands together.

Chord Caper

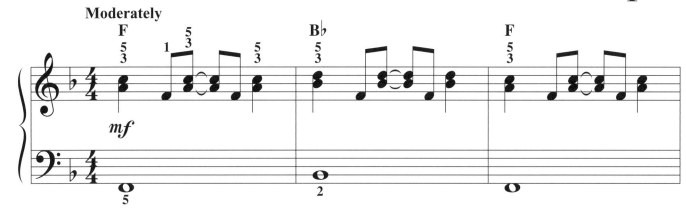

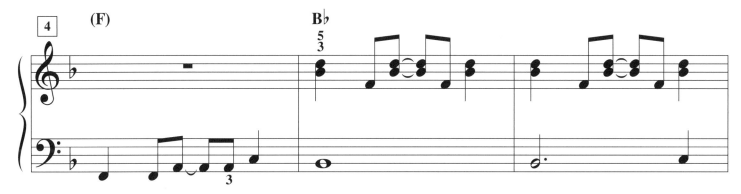

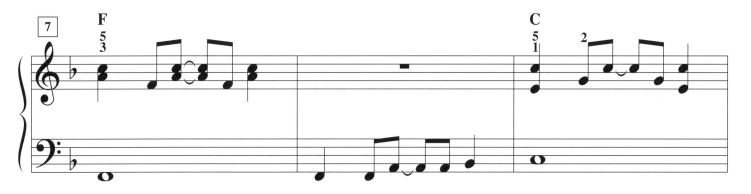

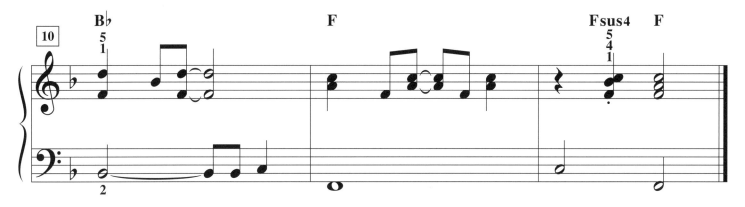

The Londonderry Air is a 17th-century Irish folk melody. It has been put to song with countless lyrics, including the highly popular *Danny Boy*, penned in 1913. The plaintive melody, often played on bagpipes, has been heard at the memorial service of John F. Kennedy and at ceremonies honoring heroic police officers and firefighters.

Directions

■ First play the melody alone, carefully observing the fingering.

■ Then add L.H. **blocked chords** on *beat 1* of each measure, as indicated by the chord symbols. (See next page.)

Notice there is no chord on the opening *upbeats*.

The Londonderry Air

Key of F Major
Lead Sheet

Traditional

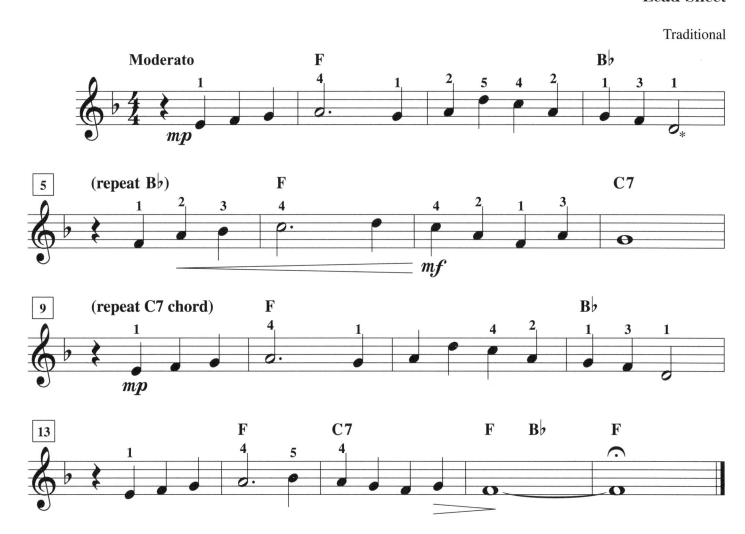

*Release the L.H. thumb (of the B♭ chord) for the melody note D.

pianoadventures.com/adult

Chord References

Practice the chords used in *The Londonderry Air*.

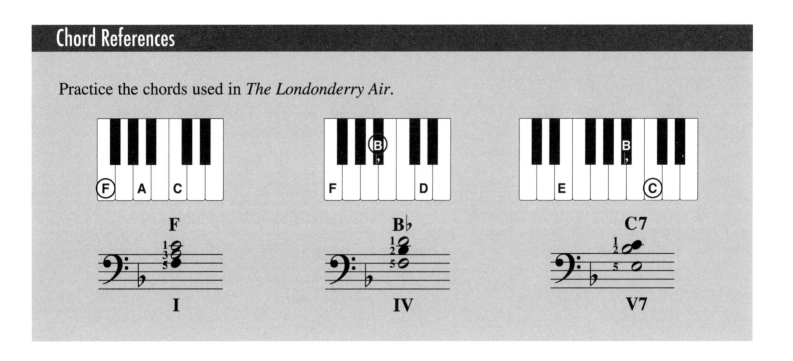

Broken-5th Accompaniment

When you can comfortably play the melody for *The Londonderry Air* with **blocked chords**, practice the melody with this L.H. accompaniment pattern.

Note: Begin each accompaniment pattern after the opening upbeats (E F G).
    Play with pedal.

Example:

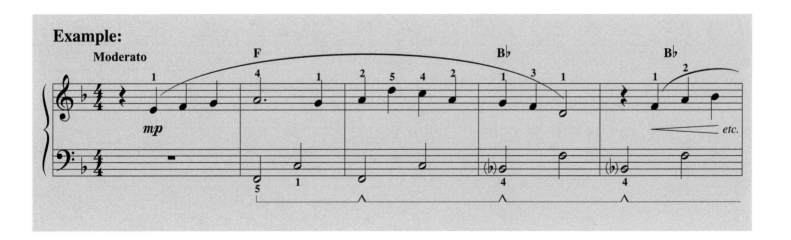

Major and Minor Triads

Major and Minor 3rds

A **major 3rd (M3)** = 4 half steps
(or two whole steps)

A **minor 3rd (m3)** = 3 half steps
(whole step plus a half step)

■ Find and play these **major 3rds**:

D, up a major 3rd to _____?

F, up a major 3rd to _____?

■ Find and play these **minor 3rds**:

G, up a minor 3rd to _____?

E, up a minor 3rd to _____?

Review: A triad is a 3-note chord built in 3rds.

A *major* triad has a **M3** between the root and 3rd.

A *minor* triad has a **m3** between the root and 3rd.

Major and Minor Triads

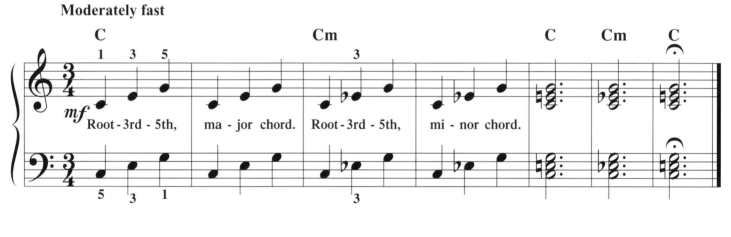

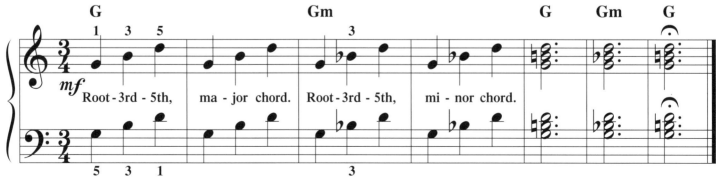

pianoadventures.com/adult

■ Continue this pattern with these **major** and **minor** chords:*

*Compare the black/white patterns of D, A, E and D♭, A♭, E♭ chords.

Unit 4: Major and Minor Triads　45

The malagueña is a colorful Spanish folk dance in rapid triple time. Originating in the provinces of Málaga and Murcia, it is often accompanied by guitars and castanets.

■ Write the letter name of each triad in the box given.
Be sure to indicate minor with a lowercase m.

Malagueña

Traditional theme
arranged

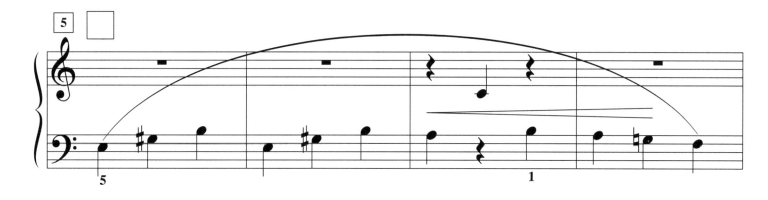

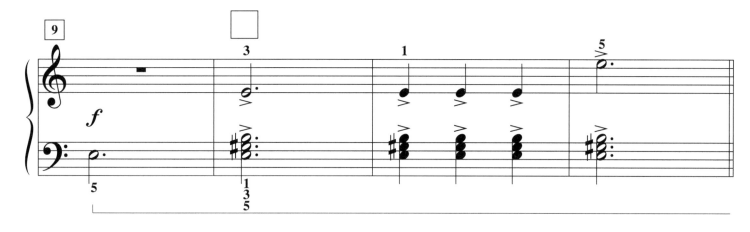

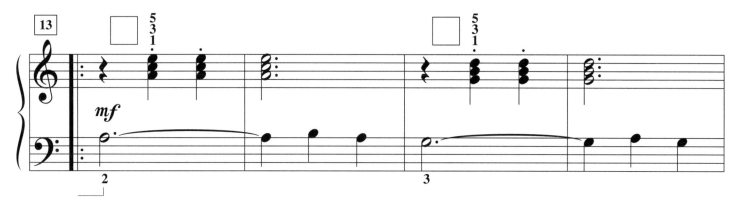

pianoadventures.com/adult

Triads on the C Major Scale

Primary chords: In a major key, the **I**, **IV**, and **V** chords are **major** triads.

Secondary chords: In a major key, the **ii**, **iii**, and **vi** chords are **minor** triads.

■ Play the triads below and listen to the *major* and *minor* sounds.

Note: The **vii** chord is neither major nor minor. It is *diminished*—comprised of two minor 3rds. (Diminished chords are indicated by a superscript °)

chord letter names:	C	Dm	Em	F	G	Am	B dim	C
chord functions:	I	ii	iii	IV	V	vi	vii°	I
chord quality:	Major	minor	minor	Major	Major	minor	diminished	Major

Long, Long Ago
Key of ____ Major

Words and Music by
Thomas H. Bayly

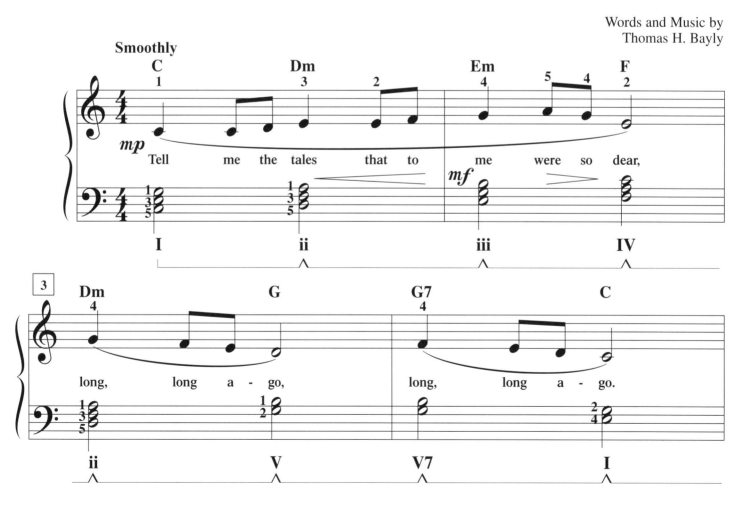

pianoadventures.com/adult

Chord Technique Hints

For full, rich chords, "cushion" the weight of your arm with a slight *down-up* motion of the wrist.

As you play each chord, let your wrists dip slightly, then return to position. The arrows indicate this *down-up* motion.

Hint: Begin with thumbs perched on the *side tips*.

■ Practice and memorize the major triads below.

Major Triads

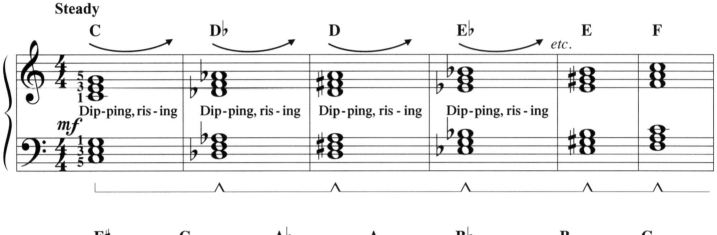

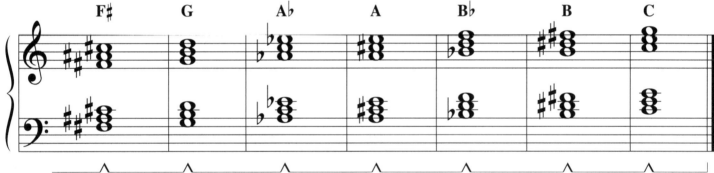

■ Play *variations* on the triad exercise above using the following two patterns:

1. Broken-Chord Variation

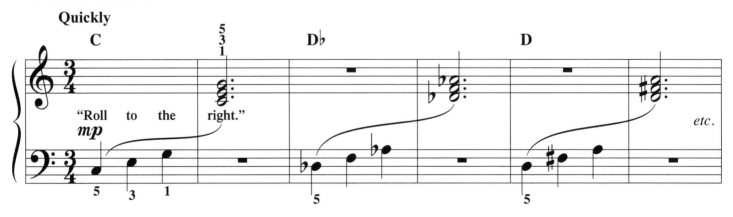

Continue this pattern moving up by half steps (E♭-E-F-F♯-G-A♭-A-B♭-B-C).

pianoadventures.com/adult

2. L.H. Octave Variation

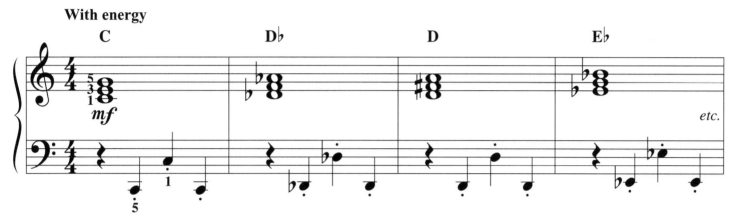

Continue this pattern moving up by half steps.

■ Practice and memorize the *minor* triads below.
Then play the two variations presented, using *minor* triads.

Minor Triads

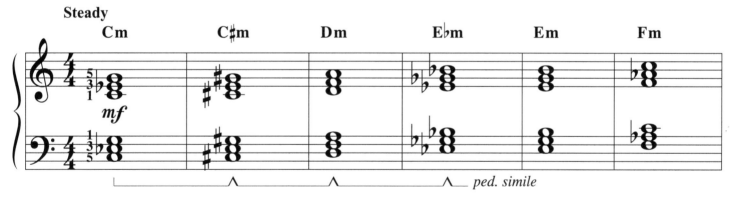

This Civil War song, long popular with barbershop quartets and college glee clubs, had been set to new lyrics as the West Point class song *Army Blues*, and much later as the Elvis Presley hit *Love Me Tender*.

Directions

- First, play the melody with pedal.
  At *measures 9–11*, the melody is shown in *octaves*.
  Keep your wrist relaxed and flexible.

- Then add L.H. **root position** chords on *beat 1* of each measure.
  (A chord reference is provided on the next page.)

Aura Lee

Key of F Major
Lead Sheet

Music by George R. Poulton
(1825–1867)

Words by William Whiteman Fosdick
(1825–1862)

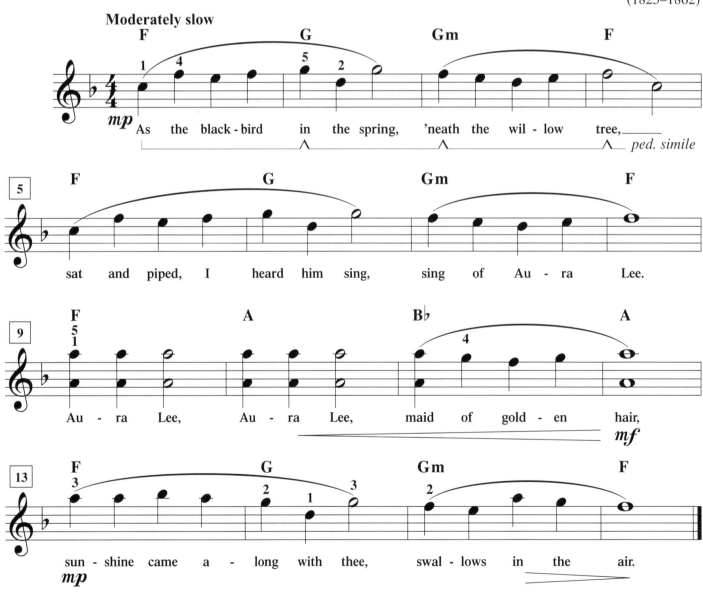

pianoadventures.com/adult

Chord References

Practice the chords used in *Aura Lee*.

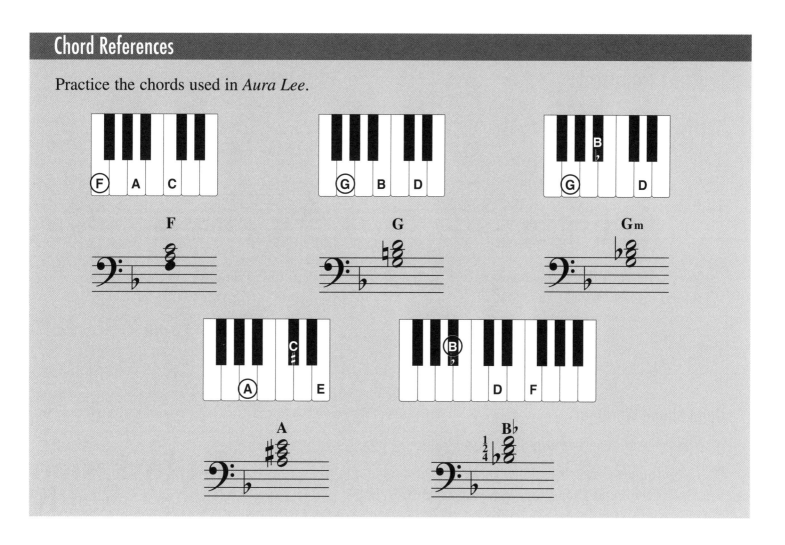

Broken-Chord Accompaniment

When you can comfortably play *Aura Lee* with **blocked chords**,
use the **broken chord** accompaniment below.

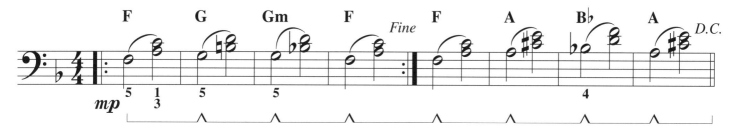

Example:

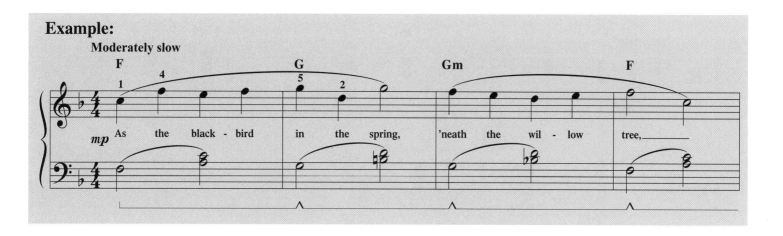

Triad Inversions

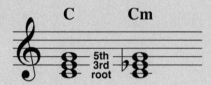

Root Position

The three notes of a triad are the **root**, **3rd**, and **5th**.

C	Cm
5th 3rd root	

When the **root** is the *lowest* note, the chord is in ROOT POSITION.

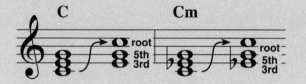

1st Inversion

The notes of a triad can be *inverted*. (The letter names stay the same.)

C	Cm
root 5th 3rd	root 5th 3rd

When the **3rd** is the *lowest* note, the chord is in 1st INVERSION.

Notice the interval of a **4th** (G up to C). The root is the *top note* of the 4th.

Hand Shape Warm-up

■ Open the R.H., extending between thumb and finger 2.

■ Keep fingers 2-3-4-5 together and round the hand slightly. This is the hand shape for 1st inversion chords.

1st Inversion Study

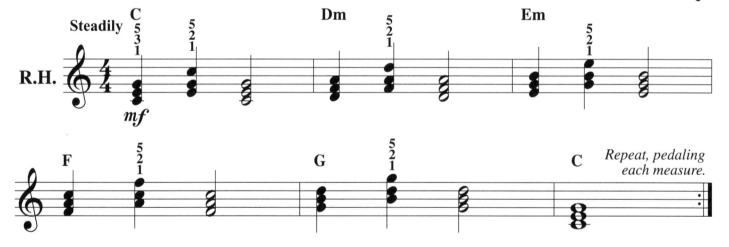

■ Repeat *Hand Shape Warm-up* with your L.H.

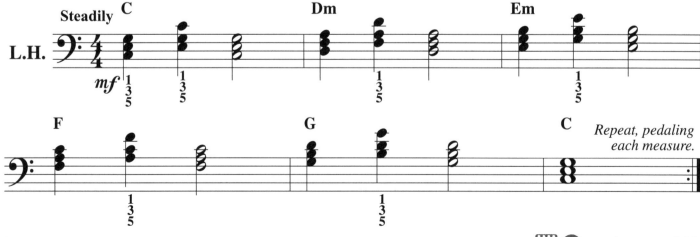

In *Westminster Chimes*, the right hand plays the melody using **1st inversion triads**.

◼ As preparation for 1st inversion triads, play the opening measures using **6ths**.

Technique Hints

◼ Keep your right hand "molded" in a
1st inversion hand shape.

◼ Your wrist should stay relaxed and flexible.

Westminster Chimes

Traditional

Joyously, slowly (♩ = 66-72)

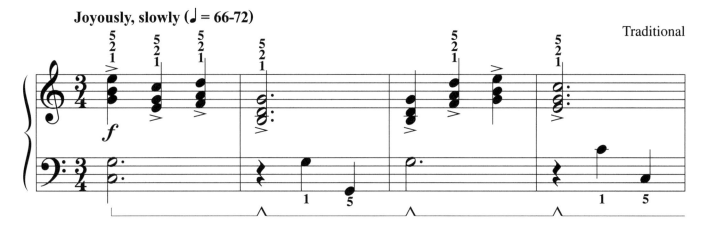

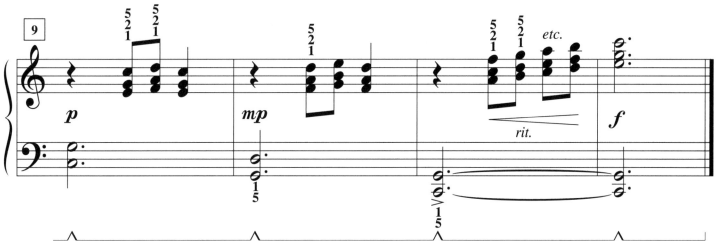

DISCOVERY   Explore the *Westminster Chimes* with R.H. playing 1 octave *higher*.
Listen to the ringing sound!

Three Positions for Triads

Every triad has 3 positions: **root position**, **1st inversion**, and **2nd inversion**.
Play these 3 positions for the C major triad. *Listen* to the sound.

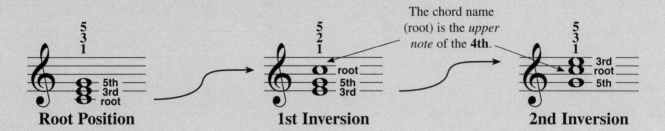

Root Position	1st Inversion	2nd Inversion
The **root** is the lowest note.	The **3rd** is the lowest note.	The **5th** is the lowest note.

The chord name (root) is the *upper note* of the 4th.

2nd Inversion Study

■ Notice the R.H. fingering and the *feel* of each chord position as you play.

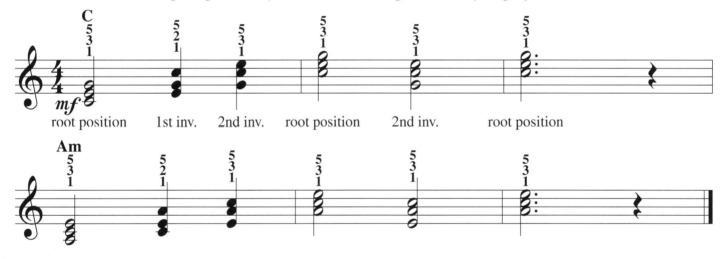

■ Notice the L.H. fingering and the *feel* of each chord position as you play.

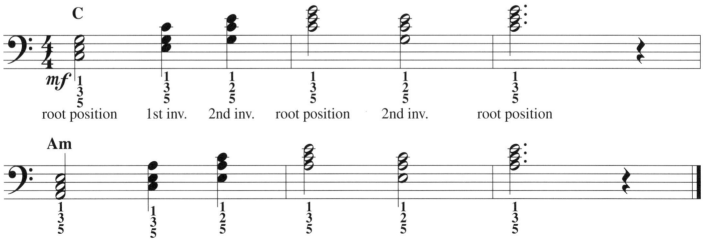

  DISCOVERY   Play *2nd Inversion Study* using **F major** and **D minor** triads.

pianoadventures.com/adult

A *gavotte* is a French dance from the 17th century.
It is danced at a moderate tempo in $\frac{4}{4}$ time.

Gavotte

Benjamin Carr
(1768-1831, U.S.A.)
original form

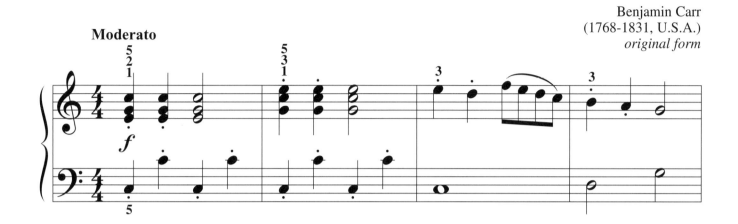

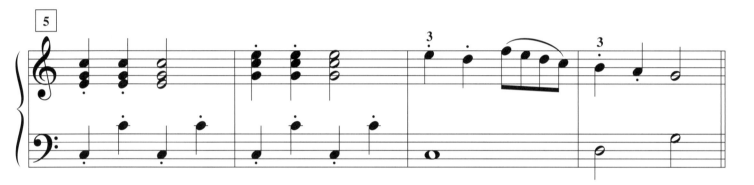

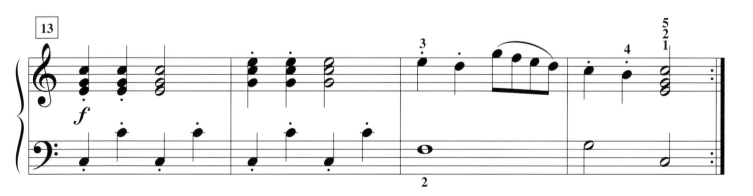

 DISCOVERY   Name the R.H. chord inversions used in *measures 1–2.*

Originating as plantation work songs, African-American spirituals typically express hope in God and freedom from the burdens of slavery. The inspiration for *Swing Low, Sweet Chariot* may have come from an earlier source: an ancient African legend of a good king who was carried to heaven in a golden chariot.

Swing Low, Sweet Chariot

Spiritual

pianoadventures.com/adult

 Find *two* places where the L.H. plays the melody. What are the dynamic marks for each?

Technique Hint

■ Toss your R.H. thumb into each *accented* note.

Review: This back-and-forth tossing (rocking) motion is called **rotation**.
　　　Keep fingers 5 and 2 close to the keys.

1st Inversion Toss
(for R.H.)

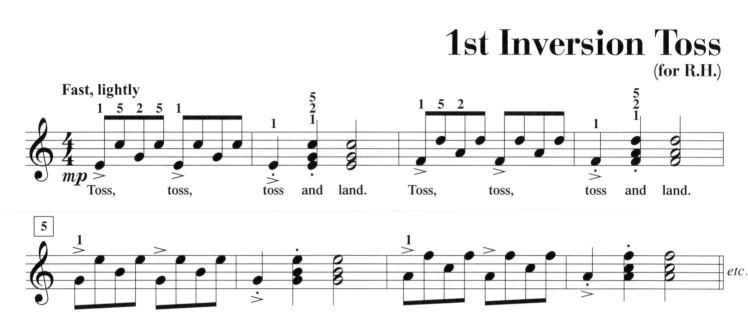

Continue this 1st inversion pattern beginning on B, C, D, and E.

Technique Hint

■ Toss L.H. finger 5 into each *accented* note using **rotation**. Keep fingers 1 and 3 close to the keys.

1st Inversion Toss
(for L.H.)

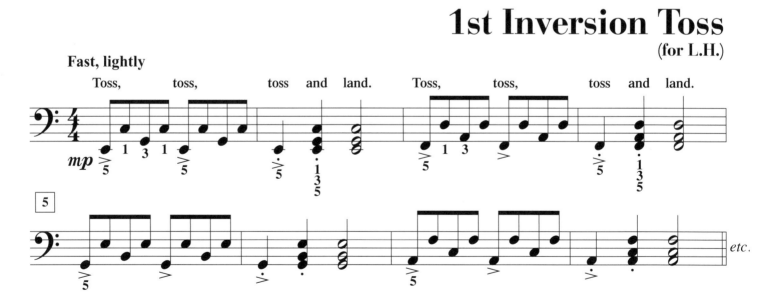

Continue this 1st inversion pattern beginning on B, C, D, and E.

Hand Shape Review

To play inversions, the hand opens by extending between the thumb and *finger 2*.
Fingers 2-3-4-5 stay together.

Sunrise
(1st and 2nd Inversions for R.H.)

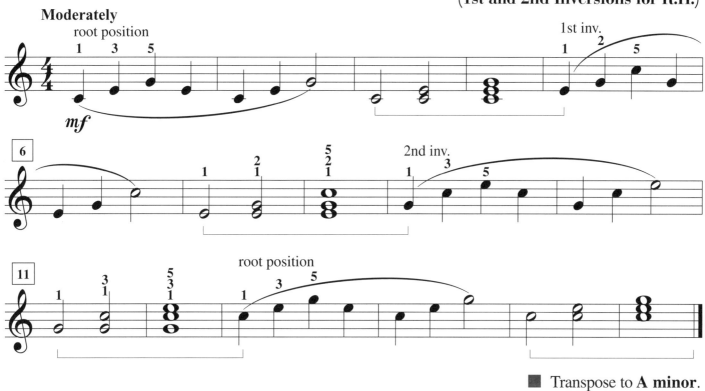

■ Transpose to **A minor**.

Sunset
(1st and 2nd Inversions for L.H.)

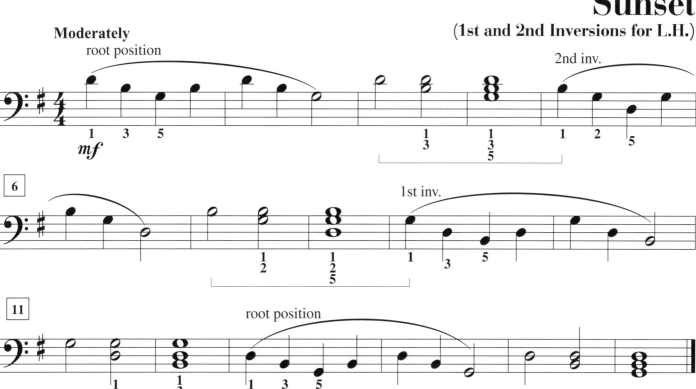

■ Transpose to **E minor**.

In this lead sheet the melody is the top note of the *1st inversion* chords.

■ Practice the R.H. alone. Keep fingers 1-2-5 in a set, molded position with your wrist relaxed.

Song of Joy

Ludwig van Beethoven
(1770–1827)

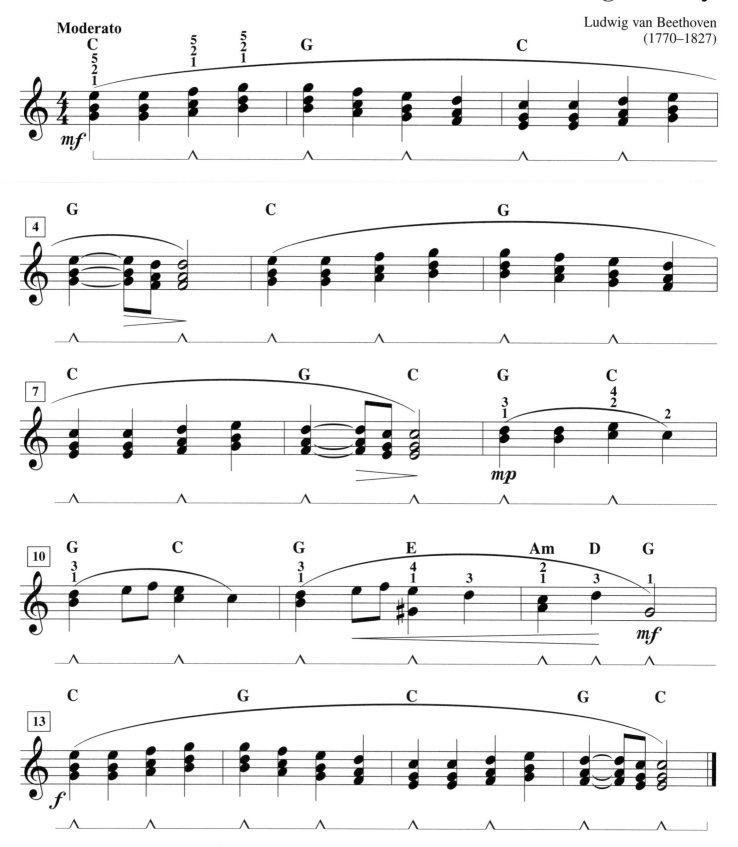

pianoadventures.com/adult

Accompanying with Chord Roots

Playing only the root of each chord can be a simple and effective L.H. accompaniment.
This is similar to the bass guitar part in a pop, rock, or jazz ensemble.

Directions

Harmonize *Song of Joy* with your L.H., playing only the **root** of each chord.

■ First, practice the **L.H. accompaniment** as shown below.
(You might enjoy *singing* the melody while you play only the L.H. bass.)

■ When ready, play the R.H. as written (p. 62) while your L.H. accompanies
using **chord roots**. (Follow the chord symbols shown above the melody.)

Song of Joy
Left-Hand Accompaniment

Eighth Rest

Eighth Rest

♪   **eighth note = 1/2 beat**   𝄿   **eighth rest = 1/2 beat**

Tap this rhythm as you count aloud, "*1 and 2 and 3 and 4 and.*"
Tap at three *tempi*: slow, medium, then fast.

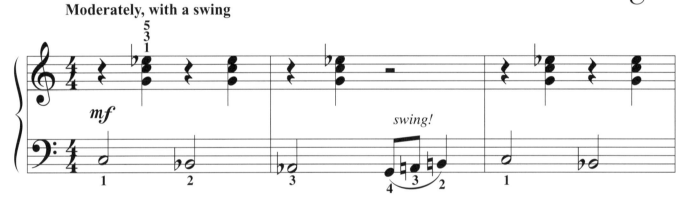

Count: 1 (+) 2 (+) 3 (+) 4 (+)   1 + 2 + 3 (+) 4 (+)

■ Practice the R.H. alone for *measures 5* and *6*
   at a **slow**, **medium**, then **fast** tempo.

Coffee House Boogie

Moderately, with a swing

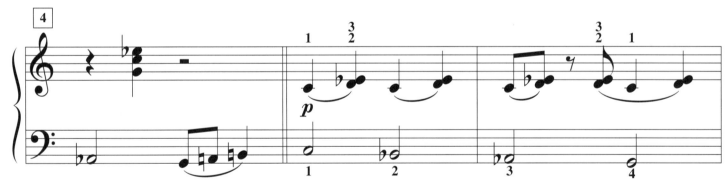

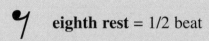 pianoadventures.com/adult

DISCOVERY Name the opening chord. Is it major or minor?

Syncopation

Syncopation occurs when notes are accented
BETWEEN the beats instead of ON the beat.

Amen

Key of ___ Major

■ Notice the syncopation that occurs in *measure 1* and repeats throughout.

The accent is on the
weak part of beat 2.

With a lively swing

Traditional

pianoadventures.com/adult

Key change
The natural cancels the B♭.

DISCOVERY   Write **Roman numerals** I, IV, or V7, below the L.H. for *measures 10-12*.

The Alberti Bass

The Alberti bass is a L.H. **broken chord** pattern named after the Italian composer Domenico Alberti.

1. In the Key of F, play a blocked **I chord** (F) with your L.H. Then play the notes separately in this order, saying aloud:

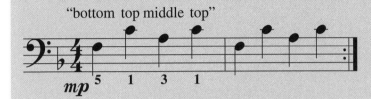

2. Play a blocked **IV chord** (B♭) with your L.H. Then play the Alberti bass example below.

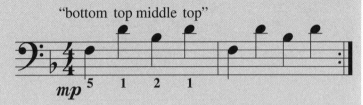

3. Play a blocked **V7 chord** (C7) with your L.H. Then play the Alberti bass example below.

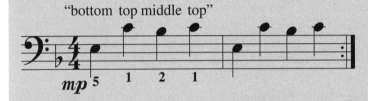

4. Play the Alberti bass example below using the alternate **V7 chord** (C7).

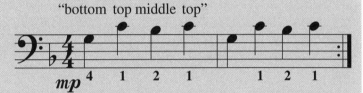

5. Now play the Alberti bass using **I**, **IV**, and **V7** chords. (Use **rotation**.)

■ Before playing, scan the music and observe the musical form.

Looking Glass River

Key of ____ Major

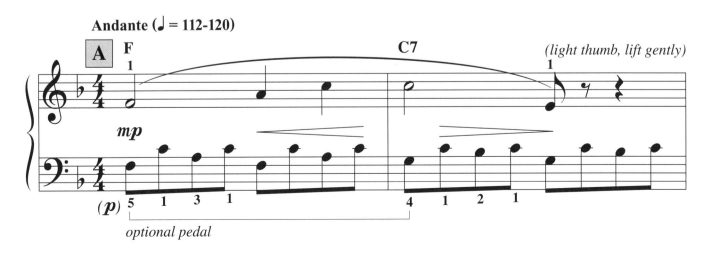

🔊 pianoadventures.com/adult

DISCOVERY

The form of this piece is **A A¹ B A¹**.
Label the harmony of the **B** section using Roman numerals (**I, IV, V7**).

- First, play the L.H. alone until the Alberti bass feels comfortable. Rotate to the first note of each grouping.

- Then, play hands together at an *andante* tempo.

Alberti Bass Study

- Transpose *Alberti Bass Study* to the **Key of G Major.**

pianoadventures.com/adult

Scale Hints

■ Play each scale with a rounded, cupped hand and firm fingertips.

■ Play the thumb *lightly* as it passes under (to prevent an accent).

Eighth-Rest Study

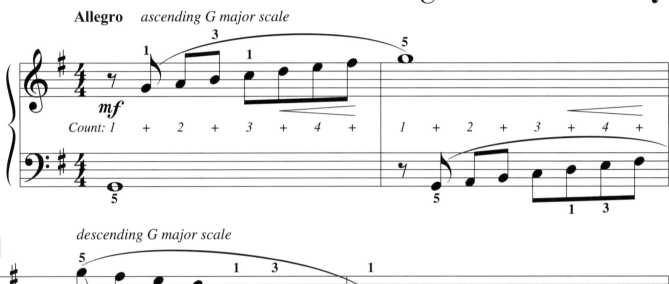

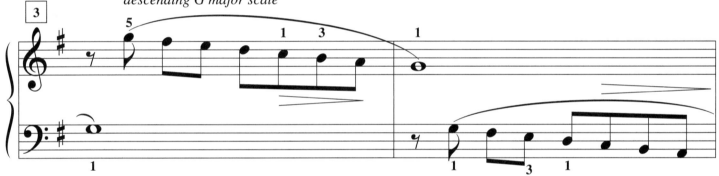

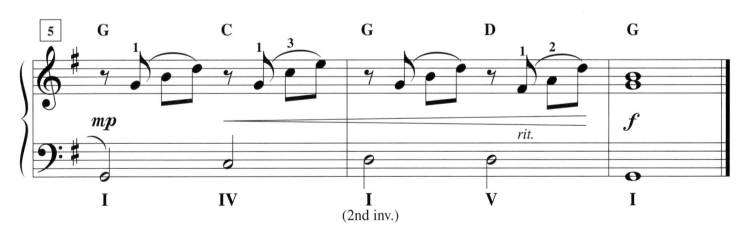

■ Transpose *Eighth-Rest Study* to the **Key of F Major.**
Hint: Remember the R.H. scale fingering for F major:
1 - 2 - 3 - 4 - 1 - 2 - 3 - 4.

Chord Symbol Review

A capital letter indicates a MAJOR chord.

For example: **G** = G major chord (G-B-D)

■ Play

In **major** chords, from root to 3rd is the interval of a **major 3rd** (4 half steps).

A capital letter plus lower-case "m" indicates a MINOR chord.

For example: **Gm** = G minor chord (G-B♭-D)

■ Play

In **minor** chords, from root to 3rd is the interval of a **minor 3rd** (3 half steps).

Primary chords

In a major key, the **I**, **IV**, and **V** chords are MAJOR triads.

Secondary chords

In a major key, the **ii**, **iii**, and **vi** chords are MINOR triads.

Triads on the G Major Scale

■ Play the **I**, **IV**, and **V** (primary) chords and listen to the *major* sound.

■ Play the **ii**, **iii**, and **vi** (secondary) chords and listen to the *minor* sound.

■ Now play the triads going up the scale, as shown below.

chord letter names:	G	Am	Bm	C	D	Em	F♯dim	G
chord functions:	I	ii	iii	IV	V	vi	vii°	I
chord quality:	Major	minor	minor	Major	Major	minor	diminished	Major

The song *Shenandoah* probably had its origins among the working rivermen in early America. The song celebrates the Shenandoah River, named after the Indian chief Shenandoah.

Directions

- First, play the melody alone with pedal.

- Then add L.H. **blocked chords** on *beat 1* of each measure, as indicated by the chord symbols.

Use root position chords, except for the **IV chord** (C) and **V7 chord** (D7), which may be played in *close position*.

Shenandoah

Key of G Major
Lead Sheet

Traditional

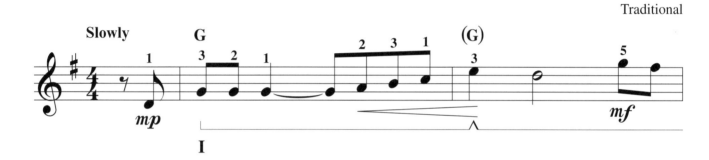

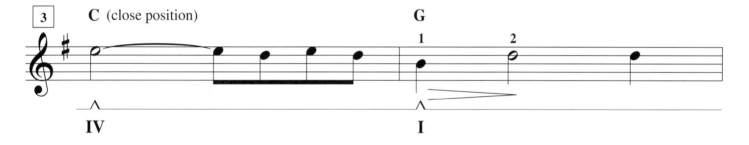

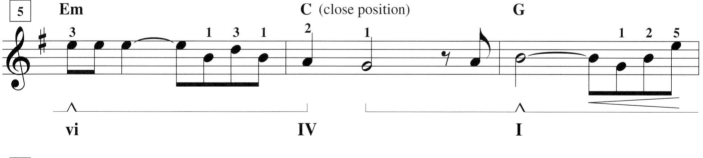

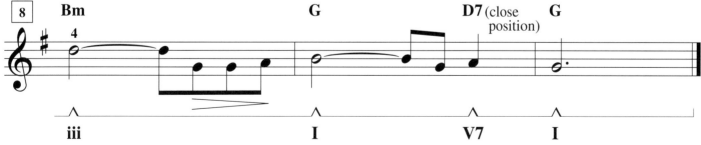

Dotted Quarter Note

■ Tap or clap the rhythms below, counting aloud.

■ Repeat, playing on an F major chord. (Play hands alone, or hands together.)

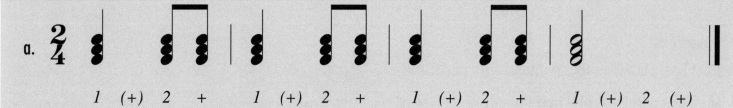

a.

1 (+) 2 + 1 (+) 2 + 1 (+) 2 + 1 (+) 2 (+)

Now **tie** the first eighth note. Feel the tied note on beat 2.

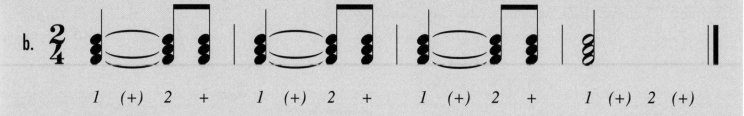

b.

1 (+) 2 + 1 (+) 2 + 1 (+) 2 + 1 (+) 2 (+)

Below, a **dot** replaces the **tied eighth note** used in the example above.
Feel the dot on beat 2! Rhythms **b** and **c** should sound exactly the same.

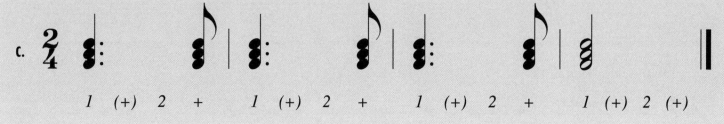

c.

1 (+) 2 + 1 (+) 2 + 1 (+) 2 + 1 (+) 2 (+)

Deck the Keys with Dotted Quarters

Brightly

Traditional melody

mf

Deck the keys with dot - ted quar - ters, fa la la la la la

la la la. 'Tis the time for dot - ted quar - ters,

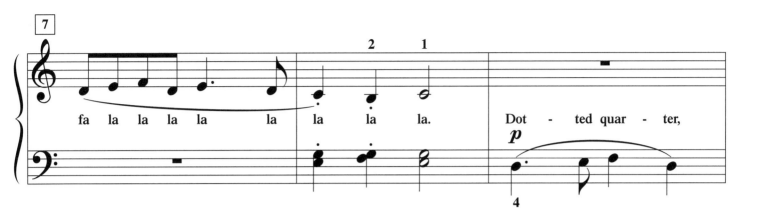

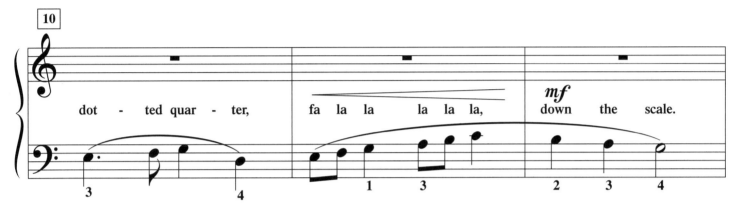

DISCOVERY

Transpose *measures 1–8* to the **Key of G**. Hint: Remember the F♯ (leading tone) when crossing the R.H. over in *measure 4* and *measure 8*.

This African spiritual has become a campfire favorite.
Kum ba yah translates to "come by here."

Kum Ba Yah

Key of _____ Major

Traditional

pianoadventures.com/adult

Write **Roman numerals** in the boxes for the chord symbols shown.
The first five measures have been done for you.

The Russian composer Rimsky-Korsakov penned this theme for his orchestral work *Scheherazade*. The composer took his inspiration from an exotic tale of a young woman named Scheherazade, as told in *The Arabian Nights*.

Arpeggiated (rolled) chord

Play the notes quickly, from bottom to top.
Use a slight upward motion of the wrist.

Theme from Scheherazade

Key of _____ Major

Nicolai Rimsky-Korsakov
(1844–1908, Russia)
arranged

*Allegretto—cheerful; rather fast (a tempo mark between *Moderato* and *Allegro*)

pianoadventures.com/adult

DISCOVERY The form of this piece is **A A¹ *Coda***.
Label each section in your music.

Practice Suggestions

- Practice the L.H. alone until you can play the chord changes easily.

- Next, mark the first R.H. slur as Pattern I. Mark the other identical patterns.

- Now play with a steady groove.

In My Red Convertible

Key of ___ Major

pianoadventures.com/adult

Get a bur - ger down on Main, cruise in, cruise

(prepare L.H.) move move

on.

mp

 DISCOVERY Can you play this song at a slow tempo using **swing rhythm**?

Duet: (Student plays *as written*)

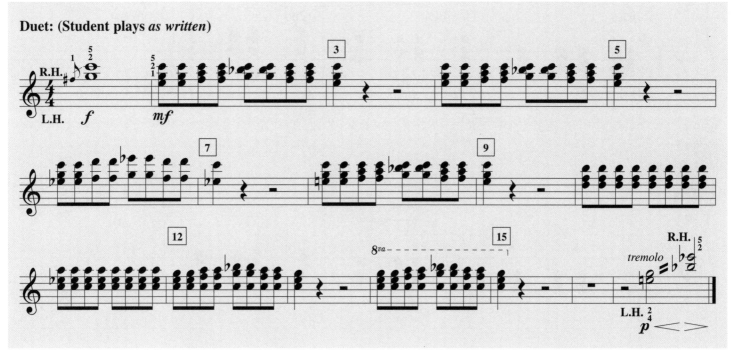

L.H. Technique Hint

■ Use a quick "up-motion" on beat 4 to carry the hand to the next inversion.

Dotted-Quarter March
G Major Primary Chords and Inversions

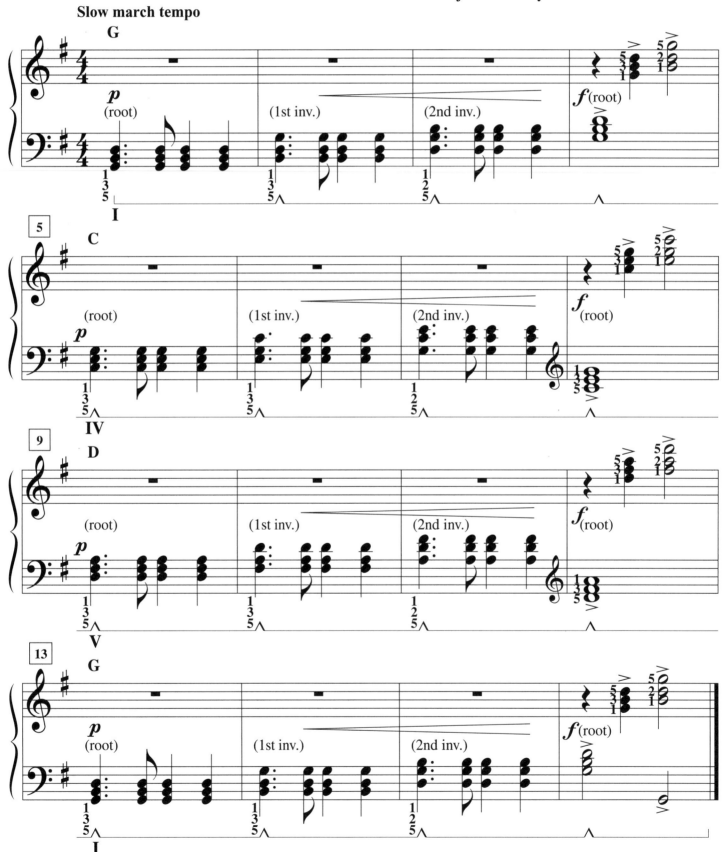

pianoadventures.com/adult

Technique Hint

■ Think of each measure as one smooth gesture of
the hand, rather than separate, individual notes.

Dotted-Quarter Arpeggios

Literally translated as "old long since," *Auld Lang Syne* continues to conclude many a New Year's Eve gathering. The song has Scottish origins, with similar words dating to 1711. A number of melodies had been paired with the text, until Robert Burns published *A Select Collection of Original Scottish Airs*, which established the current version of the song in 1798.

Directions

■ First play the melody alone with pedal.

■ Then add L.H. **blocked chords** on *beat 1* of each measure, as indicated by the chord symbols. (See next page.)

Auld Lang Syne

Key of C Major
Lead Sheet

Traditional

pianoadventures.com/adult

Chord References

Practice the chords used in *Auld Lang Syne*.

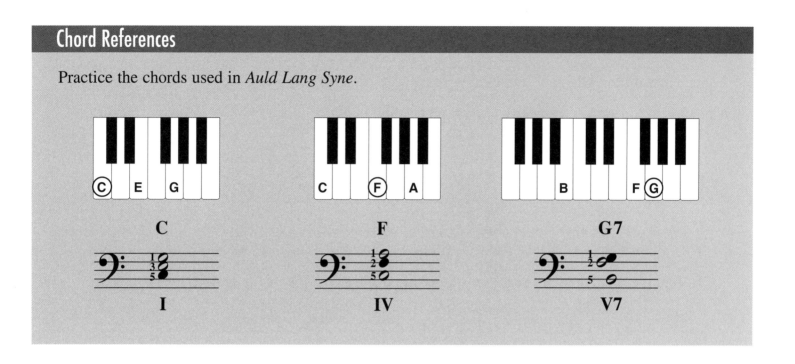

C	F	G7
I	IV	V7

Broken-Chord Accompaniment

When you can comfortably play *Auld Lang Syne* using **blocked chords**, practice accompanying the melody using **broken chords**.

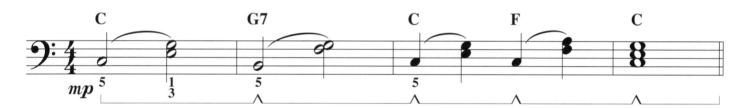

Example:

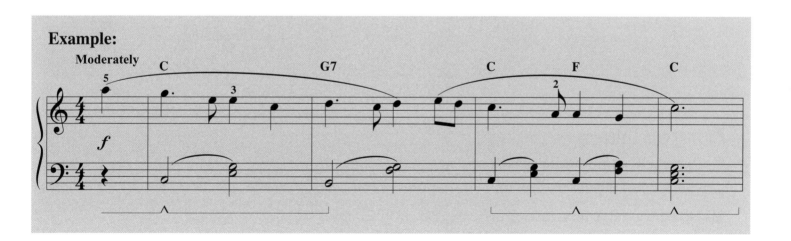

Theory of Minor Scales

A piece in a **minor key** may sound mysterious, sad, or dark.

A piece in a **major key** generally has a brighter quality.

Relative Minor Key

Every *major* key also has a *minor* key that shares the same key signature.
This minor key is called the **relative minor** because it is related by key signature.

To find the relative minor scale, start on **scale degree 6** of the major scale.

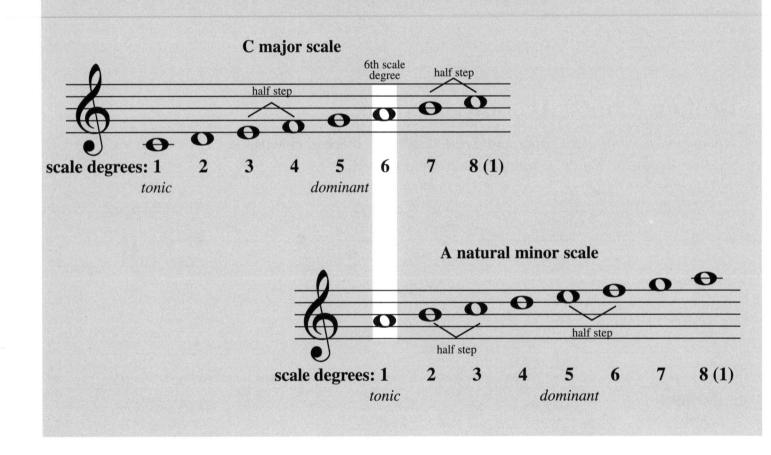

C major scale

6th scale degree   half step

half step

scale degrees: 1   2   3   4   5   6   7   8 (1)
tonic   *dominant*

A natural minor scale

half step

half step

scale degrees: 1   2   3   4   5   6   7   8 (1)
tonic   *dominant*

Playing and Listening

■ Play the **C major scale** above and listen to the sound.
The major scale has half steps between *scale degrees 3–4* and *7–8*.

■ Now play the **A natural minor scale** (the relative minor scale).
Listen to the difference in sound. The natural minor scale has half steps
between *scale degrees 2–3* and *5–6*.

Notice that the natural minor scale uses only notes from the relative major scale.

pianoadventures.com/adult

Key of A Minor

The **A NATURAL MINOR** scale shares the same key signature as the **C major scale**.

■ Notice the whole step between *scale degrees 7* and *8* in the natural minor scale.

■ Practice hands separately, then hands together.

A Natural Minor Scale

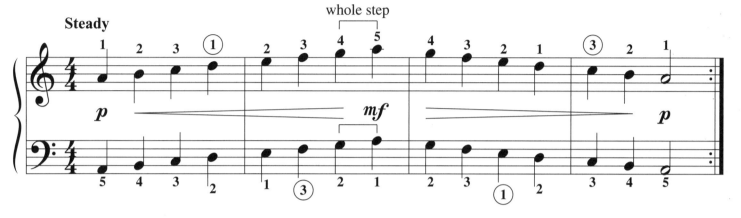

For the **HARMONIC** form of the minor scale, raise the 7th scale degree a half step.

This forms a **half step** between *scale degrees 7* and *8*, creating the *leading tone* to *tonic*.

Notice a *sharp* is needed to raise the 7th scale degree.
This sharp is not in the key signature; it is an *accidental*.

A harmonic minor scale

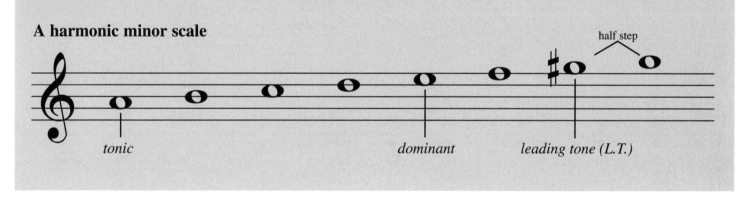

■ Practice hands separately, then hands together.

■ Listen for the *leading tone* to *tonic*.

A Harmonic Minor Scale

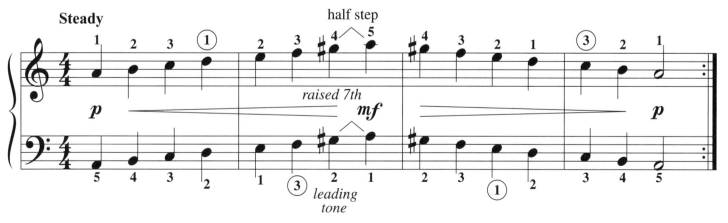

More About Key Signatures

This key signature is either **C major** or **A minor**.

A key signature indicates a **major key** or its **relative minor key**.

After recognizing the key signature in a piece, look at the *final* measure to determine the key (major or relative minor). Most pieces end on a I chord with the *tonic* note in the bass.

Ostinato

An **ostinato** is a musical pattern that is repeated over and over.

Sakura

Key of _____ Major/Minor *(circle)*

Traditional, Japan

■ Name the two intervals used for the L.H. ostinato in this piece: _____ and _____

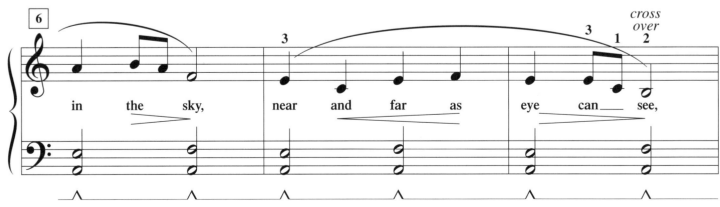

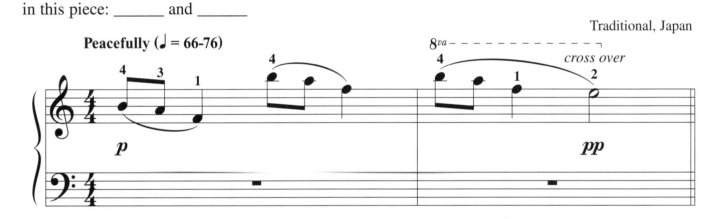

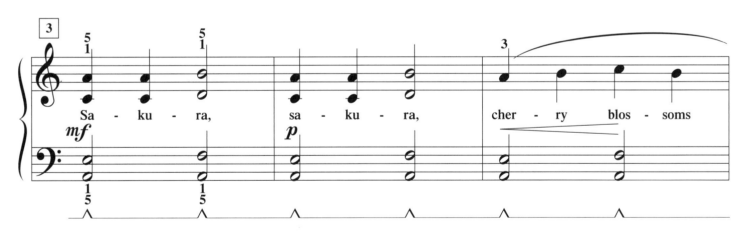

pianoadventures.com/adult

The Japanese song *Sakura* (Cherry Blossoms) celebrates the springtime flowering of the cherry blossom tree, Japan's most beloved plant and official flower.

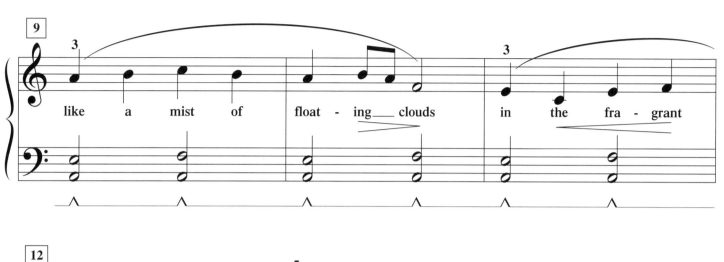

like a mist of float - ing___ clouds in the fra - grant

blush of___ spring. Come, oh come, come, oh come,

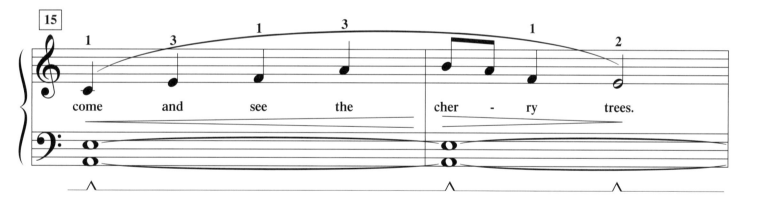

come and see the cher - ry trees.

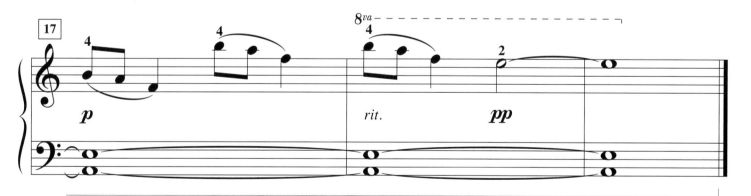

What is the final *bass* note (*lowest* note)? (*circle one*)
tonic   dominant   leading tonic

You can also quickly find the relative minor key by counting down 3 half steps from the tonic (home note) of the major key.

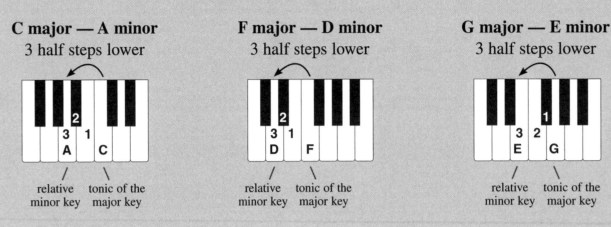

A piece in a *minor* key often has a section in the *relative major* key.

In this A minor piece, the **B section** (*m. 9*) opens in the key of C major—the **relative major**. The harmony returns to A minor at *measure 13*.

Etude in A Minor

A SECTION

A minor

Louis Köhler
(1820–1886, Germany)
original form

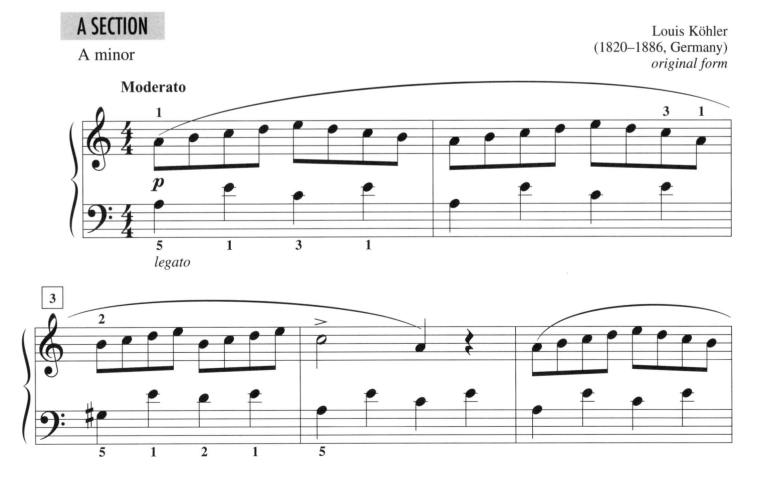

pianoadventures.com/adult

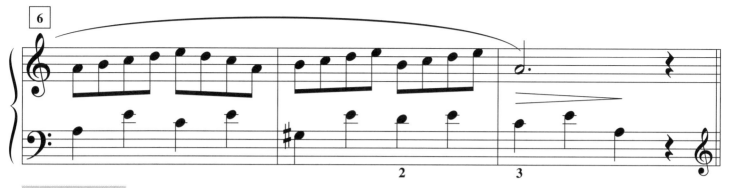

B SECTION

C major—relative major

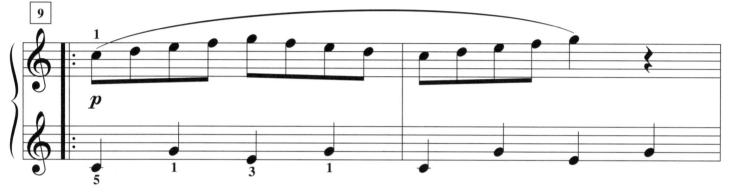

 DISCOVERY What is the name of the L.H. accompaniment pattern? _____

For a music box effect, play both hands *high* on the keyboard.

Primary Chords in A Minor: i-iv-V7

In a minor key, the **i** and **iv** chords are minor.
The **V** chord is usually major.

■ Find and play the ROOT POSITION primary chords in the **Key of A minor** shown below.
(Note: Lower-case Roman numerals may be used to indicate minor chords.)

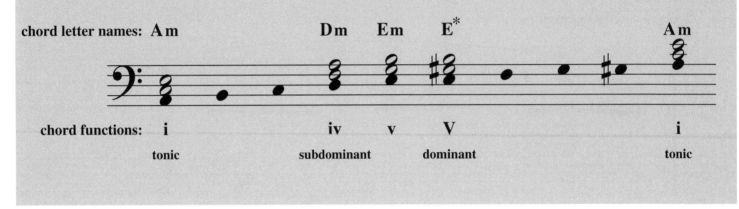

chord letter names:	A m		Dm	Em	E*				A m
chord functions:	i		iv	v	V				i
	tonic		subdominant		dominant				tonic

*The V chord is minor per the key signature, but is usually major because of the accidental from the harmonic minor scale.

Inverting the iv Chord: Dm

Review: To eliminate the leap between the **i** and the **iv** chords (**Am** chord to **Dm** chord),
the notes of the **iv** chord can be *inverted*.

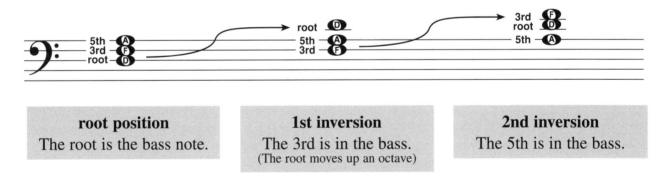

root position	**1st inversion**	**2nd inversion**
The root is the bass note.	The 3rd is in the bass. (The root moves up an octave)	The 5th is in the bass.

A Minor: i-iv Chords in Close Position

The **2nd inversion** of the **iv** chord (Dm) is often used to play **i-iv** chords in *close position*.

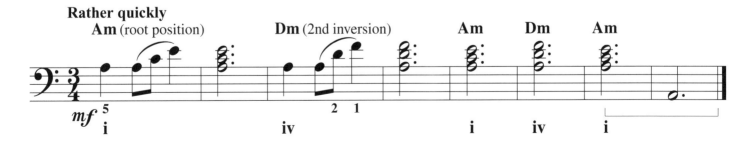

The V7 Chord in A Minor: E7

The **E7 chord** is a four-note chord built up in **3rds** from **E**.
Remember, when *E* (the root) is the *lowest* note, the chord is in root position.

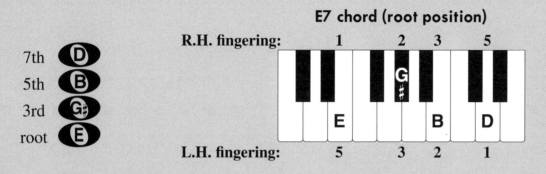

7th Ⓓ
5th Ⓑ
3rd Ⓖ♯
root Ⓔ

E7 chord (root position)

R.H. fingering: 1 2 3 5

L.H. fingering: 5 3 2 1

E is *scale degree 5* (the dominant) in the Key of A minor.
The **E7** chord is the **V7** or **dominant 7th** chord in the Key of A minor.

Inverting the V7 Chord: E7

Review: To eliminate the leap between the **i** and **V7** chords (Am to E7),
the **V7** chord is often inverted, with one of the chord tones omitted.

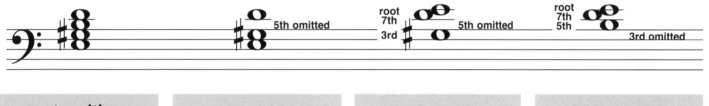

root position The root is the bass note.	**root position** with the 5th omitted (a 3-note E7 chord)	**1st inversion** The 3rd is in the bass. (the 5th is omitted)	**2nd inversion** The 5th is in the bass. (the 3rd is omitted)

A Minor: i-iv-V7 Chords in Close Position

An inversion of the **V7 chord** (E7) allows the **i-iv-V7** chords to be played in *close position*.

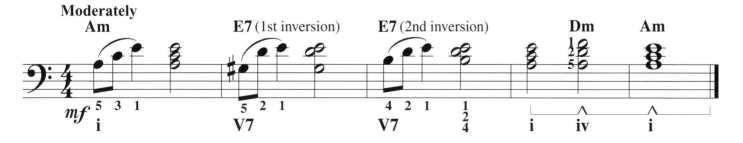

The Triplet

Sometimes **3** eighth notes equal a quarter note.
This is called a **triplet**.

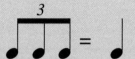

*The italic 3 indicates a triplet,
not finger number 3.*

■ Tap (or clap) and count aloud:
"*1 - and - a*" (*one-and-uh*)

1-and-a   2-and-a   3-and-a   4-and-a   1-and-a   2-and-a   3-and-a   4-and-a

---

Antonín Dvořák completed the "New World Symphony" during his first year of living in the United States, with a wildly successful New York debut in 1893. The composer reports influence from African American and Native American melodies, and proposed the idea that American concert music be based on these origins.

Finale
(from Symphony No. 9, '*From The New World*')

Key of ____ **Major/Minor**

Antonín Dvořák
(1841-1904, Bohemia)
arranged

Strong and vigorous

pianoadventures.com/adult

Label the sections of this piece **A B A**.
Then label each chord as **i**, **iv**, or **V7**.

Hava Nagila

Key of A Minor

Israeli Folk Song
arranged

pianoadventures.com/adult

 DISCOVERY Does this piece begin on the **tonic** (i) or **dominant** (V) chord?

Hand Shape Warm-up

■ Open your R.H. with the palm facing up.
Bring your fingertips and thumb together.
Notice your *cupped* hand.

■ Turn your hand over and
look for **tall knuckles**.
Repeat with the L.H.

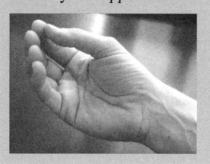
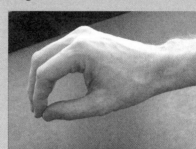

Technique Hints

■ Look for a "tall knuckle" for **finger 3**.
Play the thumb *lightly*, perched on the side tip.

■ *Listen* for even triplets that "ripple" up and down
the **A natural minor scale**.

Rippling Triplets
(for R.H.)

Rippling Triplets
(for L.H.)

pianoadventures.com/adult

Practice Suggestions

■ First, play the *broken* chords as *blocked* chords.
This will help you recognize the **i**, **iv**, and **V7** harmonies.

■ Then play as written, with pedal.

Broken-Chord Etude
Broken Chords in A Minor

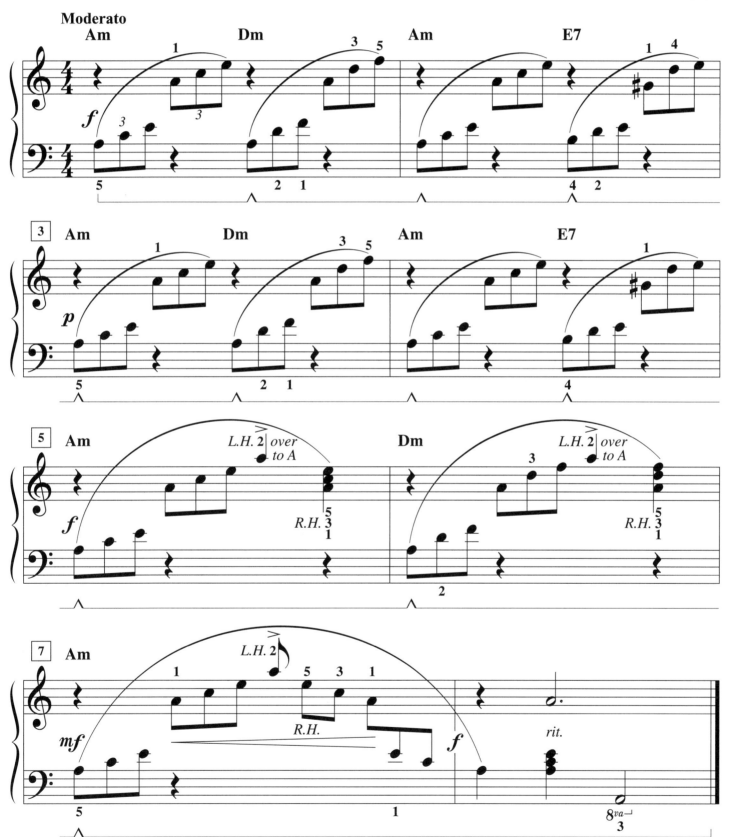

Directions

■ Play the R.H. melody alone.

■ Now add L.H. blocked chords on *beat 1* of each measure, as indicated by the chord symbols.

Notice the descending chord progression. (See next page.)

Greensleeves

Key of A Minor
Lead Sheet

The lyric of "Lady Greensleeves" dates to the 16th century. Not exactly an innocent love song, the early lyric recounts the pleading of a gentleman for love from his bored mistress. The melody was first published in 1652. Two centuries later, the Christmas carol *What Child Is This* was set to the same tune.

Chord Reference

This popular chord progression steps down from the **i chord (Am)** to the **V chord (E)**.

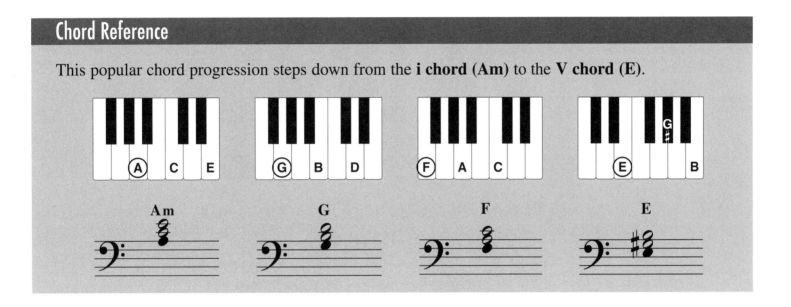

Broken-5th Accompaniment

When you can comfortably play *Greensleeves* using **blocked chords**, practice accompanying the melody using this L.H. broken-5th pattern.

Example:

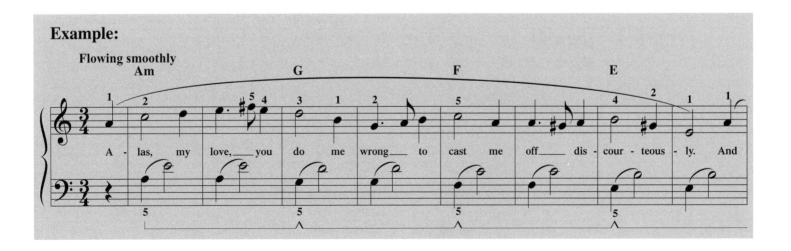

Interval of a Seventh (7th)

Interval of a 7th

The interval of a **7th** spans seven letter names (and seven white keys).

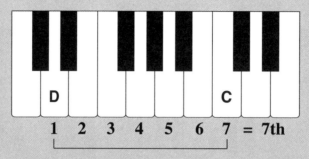

Find and play the following **7ths** on the keyboard. (Hint: A 7th is one note less than an octave.)

■ L.H. finger 5 on E. **Play up a 7th.**
   Did you land on D?

■ R.H. finger 5 on F. **Play down a 7th.**
   Did you land on G?

On the staff, a **7th** is *line to line* or *space to space*, similar to the **3rd** and **5th**.

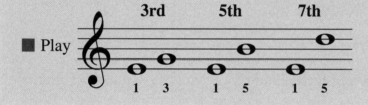

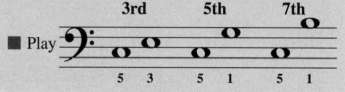

7th St. Blues

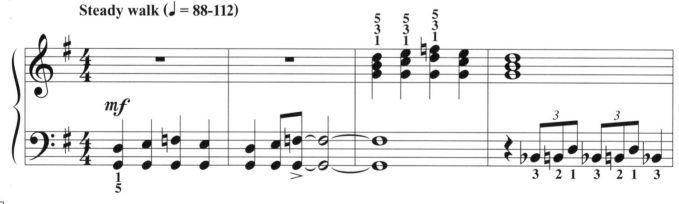

pianoadventures.com/adult

Common Time

C is the symbol for common time.
Common time is the same as $\frac{4}{4}$.

Land of the Silver Birch

Key of ____ Major/Minor *(circle)*

Folk Song of Canada
arranged

Moving gently

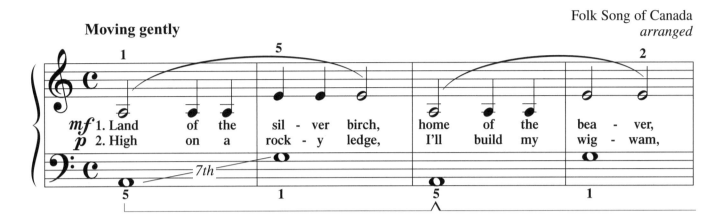

mf 1. Land of the sil - ver birch, home of the bea - ver,
p 2. High on a rock - y ledge, I'll build my wig - wam,

7th

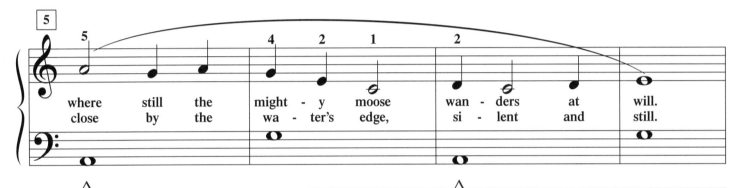

where still the might - y moose wan - ders at will.
close by the wa - ter's edge, si - lent and still.

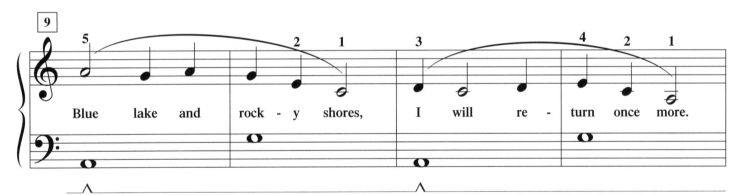

Blue lake and rock - y shores, I will re - turn once more.

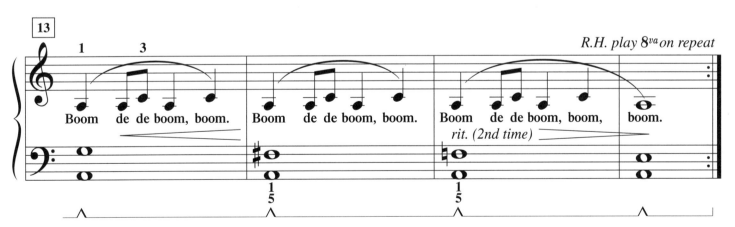

R.H. play 8va on repeat

Boom de de boom, boom. Boom de de boom, boom. Boom de de boom, boom, boom.

rit. (2nd time)

CREATIVE
Notice this piece uses a L.H. 7th as an *ostinato*.
Explore creating a short piece of your own using this ostinato.
For the R.H. melody, play notes from the **A natural minor scale**.

Cut Time ₵ = $\frac{2}{2}$

Cut time is $\frac{4}{4}$ time divided in half: $\frac{2}{2}$

It is notated the same as $\frac{4}{4}$ time, but is played with **2 beats per measure**.

The ♩ gets the beat.

Cut time is also known as *alla breve*.

■ Play quickly, feeling **2 beats** per measure.

Count: 1 and 2 and 1 and 2 and

Give My Regards to Broadway is from George M. Cohan's first original musical comedy *Johnny Jones* (1904). This musical stood in sharp contrast to other musicals of the day because of its American theme and speech.

Give My Regards to Broadway

George M. Cohan
(1878–1942, U.S.A.)
arranged

optional pedal

DISCOVERY Point out three *accidentals* in this arrangement, including a sharp, a flat, and a natural.

Technique Hint

■ Play the final *forte* chords (*m. 19*) using a slight *down-up* wrist motion. This "cushioning" motion of the wrist helps produce a full, round tone.

Note: The arrows at *mm. 19–21* indicate this motion.

Fanfare Etude

Key of _____ **Major/Minor** (*circle*)

Energetic and triumphant, "in two"

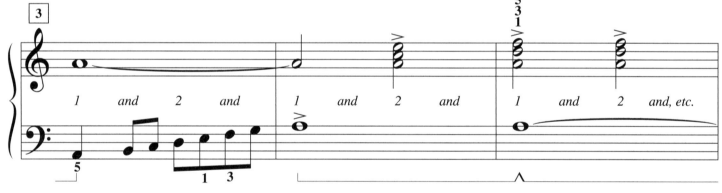

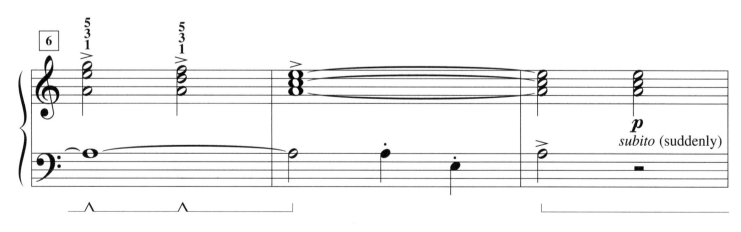

pianoadventures.com/adult

Directions

- First, play the melody alone with pedal.

- Then add **blocked chords** on *beat 1* of each measure. (N.C. means *no chord*.)

Mexican Clapping Song

C Major
Lead Sheet

Mexican Folk Song

pianoadventures.com/adult

Chord Reference

Review the chords used in *Mexican Clapping Song*.

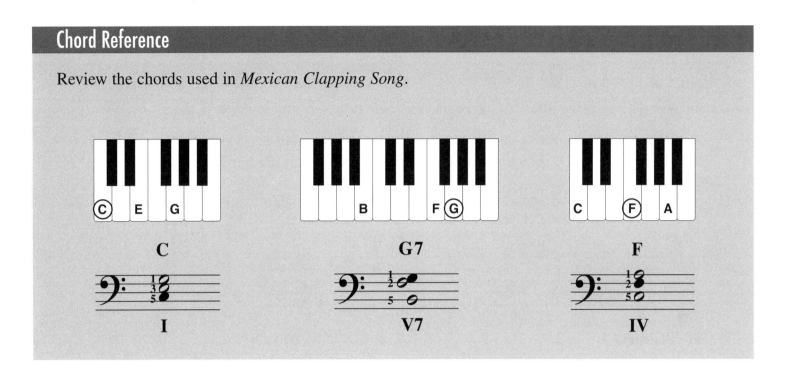

Waltz Accompaniment

When you can comfortably play *Mexican Clapping Song* using **blocked chords**, play the **B section** (*mm. 11–26*) using the L.H. **waltz accompaniment** below. (Use blocked chords for the *D.C.*)

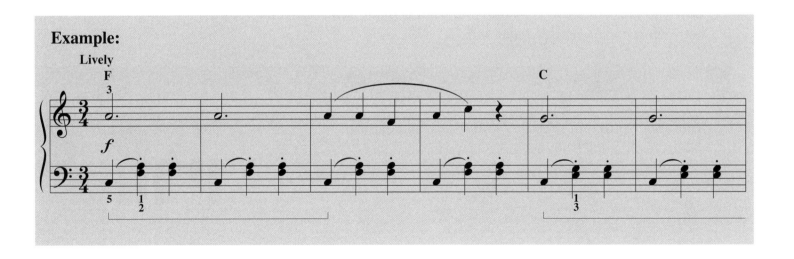

F Major and D Minor

Review: The **relative minor** scale begins on *scale degree 6* of the major scale.

New: The key of **D minor** is the RELATIVE MINOR of **F major**. (D is the 6th scale degree in the F major scale.) **D minor** and **F major** share the same key signature: one flat (B♭).

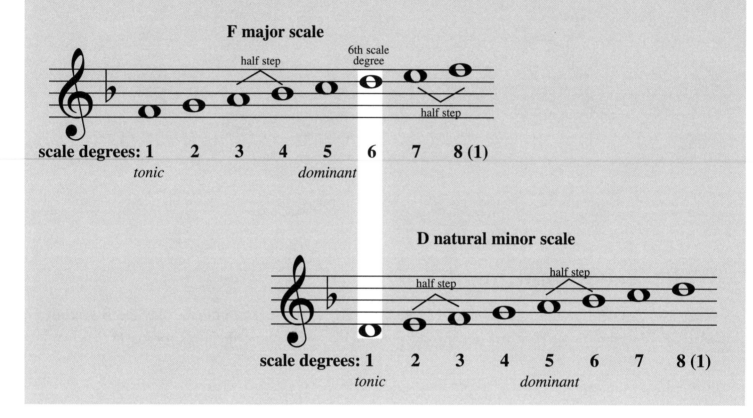

Playing and Listening

■ Play the **F major scale** and listen to the sound.
The major scale has **half steps** between *scale degrees 3–4* and *7–8*.

■ Now play the **D natural minor scale** (the relative minor scale).
Listen to the difference in sound. The natural minor scale has half steps between *scale degrees 2–3* and *5–6*.

Reminder

You can also find the **relative minor key** by counting down 3 half steps from the *tonic* of the major key.

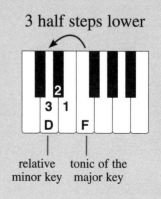

▶ pianoadventures.com/adult

The **D NATURAL MINOR** scale shares the same key signature as the **F major scale**.

■ Notice the **whole step** between *scale degrees 7* and *8* in the natural minor scale.

■ Practice hands separately, then hands together.

D Natural Minor Scale

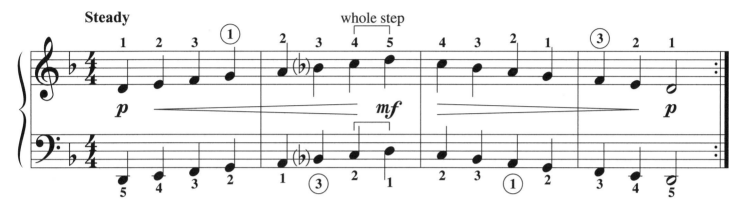

For the **HARMONIC MINOR** scale, raise the 7th scale degree a half step.

This forms a **half step** between *scale degrees 7* and *8* (leading tone to tonic).
Remember, an accidental is needed to raise the 7th scale degree.

D harmonic minor scale

scale degrees: 1	2	3	4	5	6	7	8 (1)
tonic				*dominant*		*leading tone (L.T.)*	
i				**V**			

■ Practice hands separately, then hands together.

■ Listen for the *leading tone* to *tonic*.

D Harmonic Minor Scale

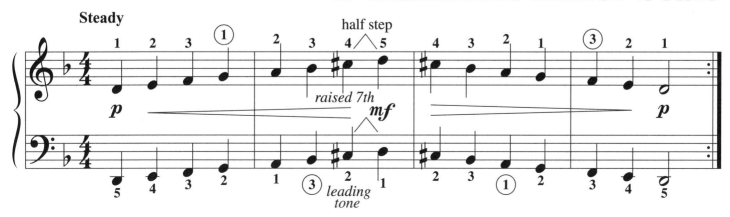

Primary Chords in D Minor: i - iv - V7

Review: In a minor key, the **i** and **iv** chords are minor.
The **V** chord is usually major.

■ Find and play the ROOT POSITION primary chords in the **Key of D minor** shown below.

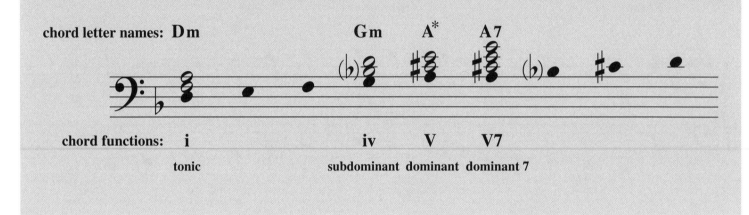

chord letter names:	Dm		Gm	A*	A7			

chord functions:	i		iv	V	V7			
	tonic		subdominant	dominant	dominant 7			

*The V chord is minor per the key signature, but is usually major because of the accidental from the harmonic minor scale.

Inverting the iv Chord: Gm

Review: To eliminate the leap between the **i** and the **iv** chords (**Dm** chord to **Gm** chord),
      the notes of the **iv** chord can be *inverted*.

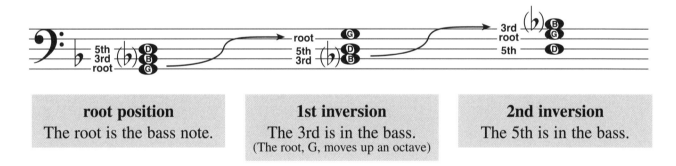

root position	**1st inversion**	**2nd inversion**
The root is the bass note.	The 3rd is in the bass.	The 5th is in the bass.
	(The root, G, moves up an octave)	

D Minor: i-iv Chords in Close Position

The **2nd inversion** of the **iv** chord (Gm) is often used to play **i-iv** chords in *close position*.

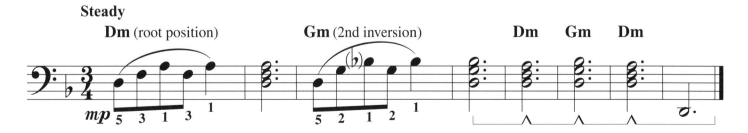

The V7 Chord in D Minor: A7

The **A7 chord** is a four-note chord built up in **3rds** from **A**.

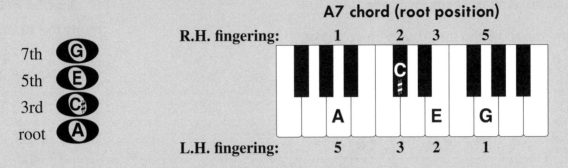

7th G
5th E
3rd C#
root A

A7 chord (root position)
R.H. fingering: 1 2 3 5
L.H. fingering: 5 3 2 1

A is *scale degree 5* (the dominant) in the Key of D minor.
The **A7** chord is the **V7** or **dominant 7th** chord in the Key of D minor.

Inverting the V7 Chord: A7

An inversion of the **A7** chord eliminates the leap between root position chords.

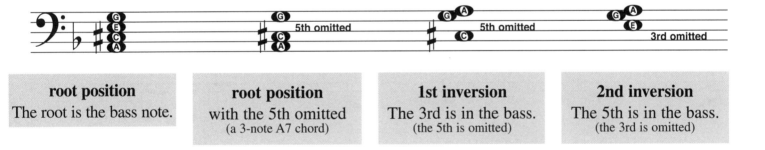

root position	**root position**	**1st inversion**	**2nd inversion**
The root is the bass note.	with the 5th omitted (a 3-note A7 chord)	The 3rd is in the bass. (the 5th is omitted)	The 5th is in the bass. (the 3rd is omitted)

D Minor: i-iv-V7 Chords in Close Position

An inversion of the **V7** chord (A7) allows the **i-iv-V7** chords to be played in *close position*.

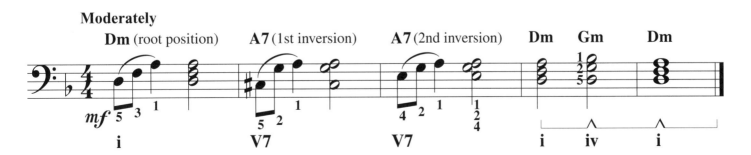

Habanera is the famous aria from Georges Bizet's opera *Carmen*. Though the opera is now considered a masterpiece, the French critics and public condemned the work and its gypsy theme. Bizet died in despair shortly thereafter. The story is set in Spain, with the habanera dance rhythm providing an exotic flair.

Habanera opens in the **Key of D minor** and changes to the **Key of D major** at *measure 10*.

The exotic mood of the minor section contrasts with the triumphant quality of the major section.

Habanera
(from the opera *Carmen*)

Georges Bizet
(1838–1875, France)
arranged

The natural cancels the B♭.

pianoadventures.com/adult

Habanera uses the primary chords in D minor (**i**, **iv**, **V7**) and
D major (**I**, **IV**, **V7**). Write the Roman numerals under the bass staff.

sfz — *sforzando*
a sudden, strong accent

This spiritual tells the story of Joshua leading the Israelites into the Promised Land. The battle of Jericho is recounted in the Old Testament of the Bible, Book of Joshua.

Joshua Fought the Battle of Jericho

Key of ____ Major/Minor

Spiritual

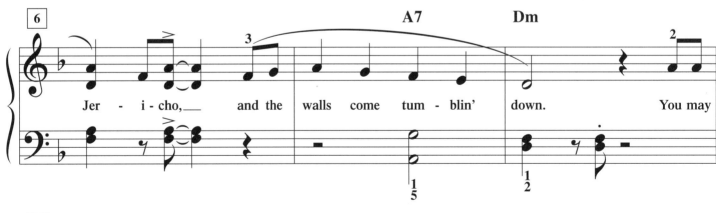

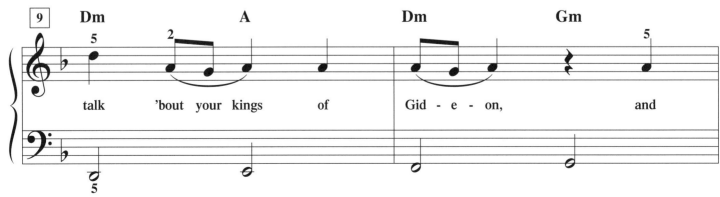

116   Unit 10: Key of D Minor

pianoadventures.com/adult

This song is in *ternary* form (**A B A** form).
Label the sections in the music.

Balance Between the Hands

■ Bring out the melody by using **arm weight**,
sinking gently to the bottom of the key.

■ Soften the accompaniment by using *less* arm weight.
Play lightly from the surface of the key.

Theme and Variations
on the D Minor Scale

pianoadventures.com/adult

When you can easily play the *theme* (page 118), learn these *variations* for more practice with **i**, **iv**, and **V7** accompaniments.

VARIATION 1: **Waltz bass pattern**

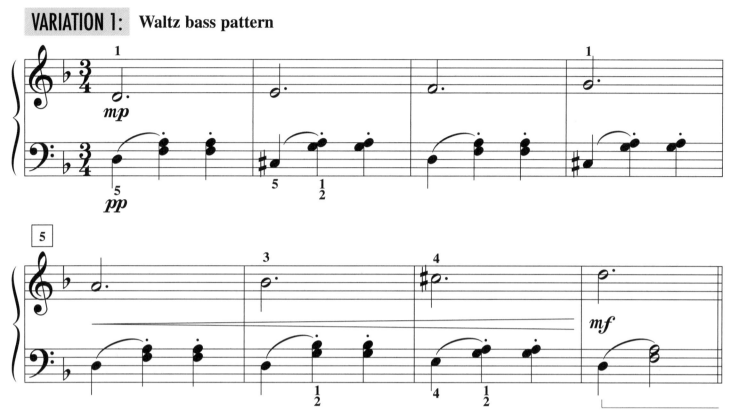

Complete Variation 1 by playing *measures 9–14* on the previous page.

VARIATION 2: **Broken chord pattern**

Complete Variation 2 by playing *measures 9–14* on the previous page.

Dark Eyes (Ochi Chiornie) is one of the most popular of Russian "Gypsy songs." Although Dark Eyes is often performed by Gypsy (Romany) musicians who take pride in their renditions of it, they are quick to point out that Dark Eyes is not a real Romany song, but was written by a Russian. Despite this assertion, the song has become synonymous with Gypsy music.

Directions

■ First, play the melody alone.

■ Then add a L.H. *staccato* **blocked chord** on *beat 1* of each measure, as indicated by the chord symbols. (See next page for chords.)

Reminder: There is no chord on the upbeats.

Dark Eyes
D minor
Lead Sheet

Traditional Russian

pianoadventures.com/adult

Chord Reference

Practice the chords used in *Dark Eyes*.

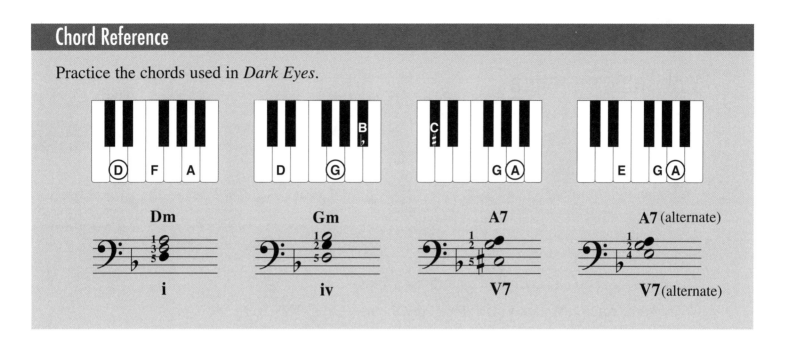

Rhythmic Chord Accompaniment

When you can comfortably play *Dark Eyes* with **blocked chords**, practice playing the melody with this L.H. accompaniment pattern.

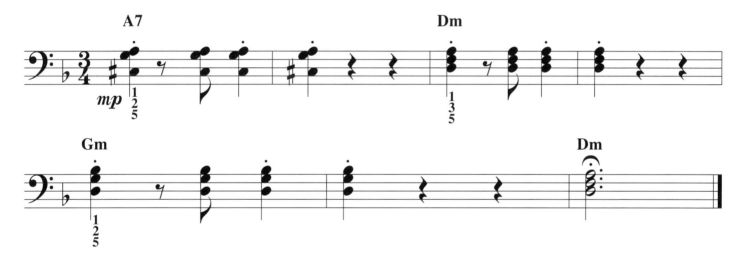

Example:

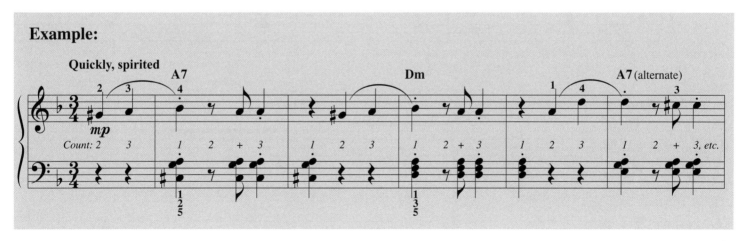

New Time Signature

$\frac{3}{8}$ —3 beats in a measure
—the eighth note ♪ gets 1 beat

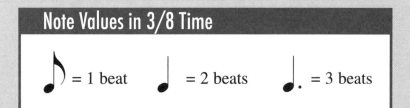

Note Values in 3/8 Time

♪ = 1 beat   ♩ = 2 beats   ♩. = 3 beats

These are some common rhythm patterns in $\frac{3}{8}$ time.

■ Tap and count. (You may wish to set the metronome at ♪ = 160.)

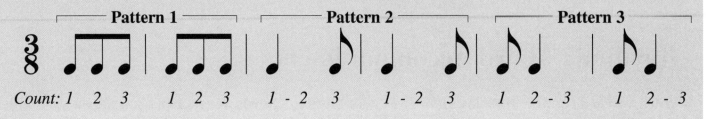

Pattern 1	Pattern 2	Pattern 3
Count: 1 2 3 1 2 3	1 - 2 3 1 - 2 3	1 2 - 3 1 2 - 3

In the various renditions of this English folk song, two qualities are always present: a list of impossible tasks for a lover to perform, and the repetition of four herbs— parsley, sage, rosemary, and thyme.

Scarborough Fair
Key of ____ Major/Minor

English Folk Song
arranged

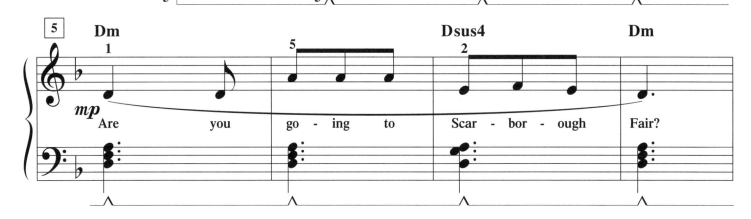

Find an example of each rhythm pattern in this piece.

New Time Signature

6 — 6 beats in a measure
8 — the **eighth note** ♪ gets one beat

The $\frac{6}{8}$ time signature is a combination of $\frac{3}{8} + \frac{3}{8}$.

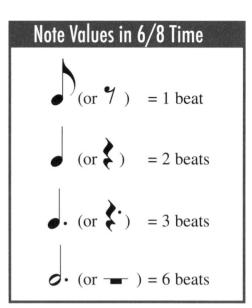

Note Values in 6/8 Time

♪ (or 𝄾)	= 1 beat
♩ (or 𝄽)	= 2 beats
♩. (or 𝄽˙)	= 3 beats
𝅗𝅥. (or ▬)	= 6 beats

■ Tap and count these $\frac{6}{8}$ rhythms (♪ = **144-160**).

■ Then play each rhythm on the chord suggested.

PATTERN 1

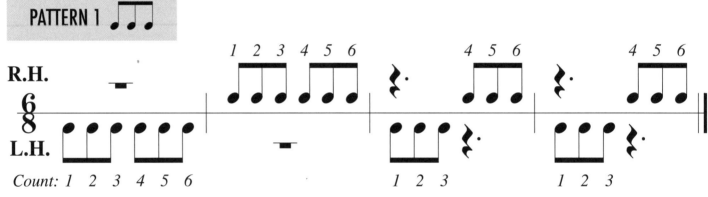

■ Now play using **C major** chords.

PATTERN 2

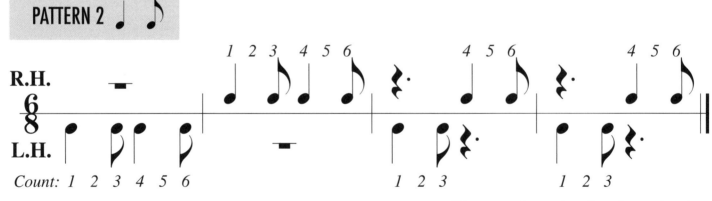

■ Now play using **D minor** chords.

PATTERN 3

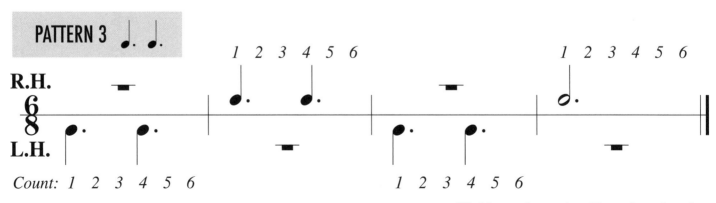

■ Now play using **F major** chords.

Familiar §8 Melodies

Each of these melodies is in §8 time.

■ Write the counts "*1 2 3 4 5 6*" under each measure.

■ Then play the melodies on the piano. Play more of the melody "by ear" if you wish.

Over the River and Through the Woods

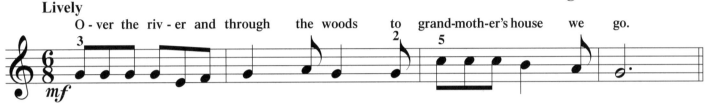

Write: 1 2 3 4 5 6

Row, Row, Row Your Boat

Write: 1 2 3

For He's a Jolly Good Fellow

Write: 6 1 2 3

Sailing, Sailing

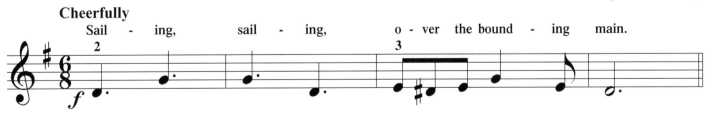

Write:

DISCOVERY   Circle this rhythm pattern in the music above: (There are 10 of these.) ♩♪

> *Campbells Are Coming* is a traditional dance tune of Scottish heritage.
> Commonly played on the bagpipes, it is usually accompanied by drone 5ths.
> The tune may have been used as a battle march by the rebelling Stuart clan
> when opposed by the Clan Campbell, who allied with the King of England.

Campbells Are Coming

Key of ____ Major/Minor

Traditional Scottish
arranged

■ Before you play, draw bar lines
for *measures 13–24.*

(draw bar lines)

Transpose this piece to the **Key of C Major**.
Hint: At *measure 9*, your L.H. will move up to an A-E 5th.

In faster tempos, $\frac{6}{8}$ is felt with **2 beats** per measure. The ♩. gets the beat.

Tap this rhythm, counting aloud.

Count: 1   2   1 and a 2

Pronounced "fu-nee-ku-lee, fu-nee-ku-lah."
This Italian song was written to celebrate the
opening of a funicular railway (a mountain
cable car) that went to the top of Mt. Vesuvius.

Funiculì, Funiculà

Key of ____ Major

Luigi Denza
(1846-1922, Italy)
arranged

■ Notice the L.H. chords mark out the two "big beats" per measure.

Moderato, "in two" (♩. = 104-120)

mf

Some   think_____   the world   is   made   for   fun   and

Count and feel: 1   2   1   2   1   2 etc.

L.H.
lightly

frol - ic,_____   and so   do   I!   And so   do

I!   Some   think_____   it well   to

be   all   mel - an - chol - ic,_____   to pine   and   sigh,

pianoadventures.com/adult

In faster tempos, $\frac{6}{8}$ is felt as:

6 beats to a measure   2 beats to a measure   *(circle one)*

■ Feel two ♩. beats per measure
for this primary chord exercise.

Chord Study "in Two"

Key of _____ Major/Minor

■ Transpose to the keys of **F major** and **C major**.

■ Notice the *andante* tempo mark. Feel this
graceful pedal study with 6 beats per measure.

Pedal Study
(for L.H. alone)

Key of _____ Major/Minor

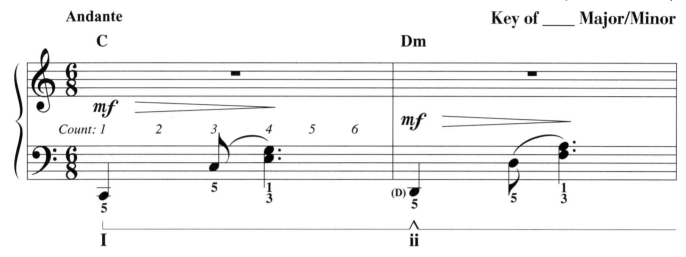

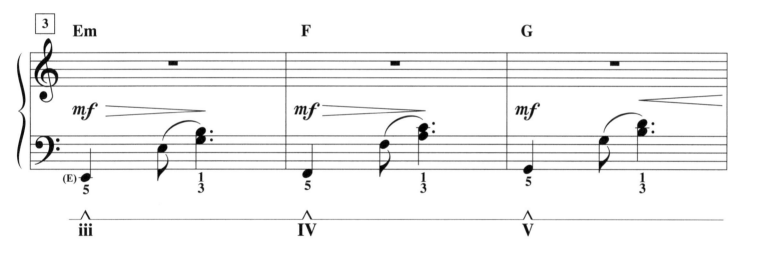

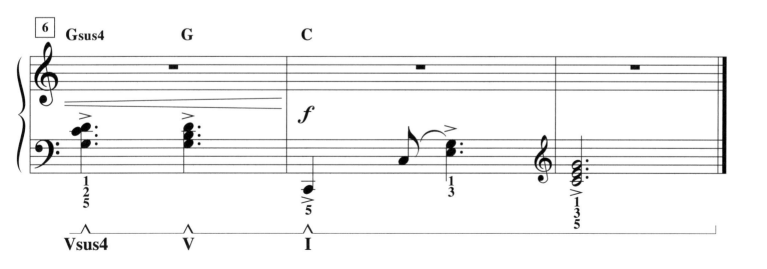

A barcarolle is a piece of music that suggests the songs sung by gondoliers as they row their gondolas on the canals of Venice. The sentimental, melancholy mood of the barcarolle has led to its frequent use in romantic opera. Perhaps, the most famous example is that of Offenbach in Act 2 of *Les Contes d'Hoffmann* (The Tales of Hoffmann).

Directions

- First, play the melody alone with pedal.

- Then add L.H. **blocked chords** on *beat 1* of each measure, as indicated by the chord symbols.

Barcarolle

(from the opera *The Tales of Hoffmann***)**

Jacques Offenbach
(1819–1880, France)

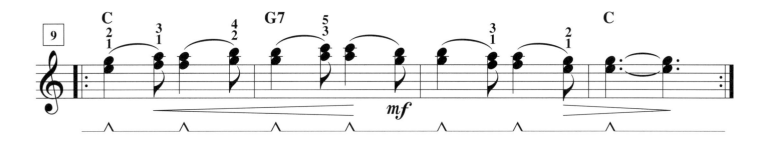

pianoadventures.com/adult

Chord Reference

Practice the chords used in *Barcarolle*.

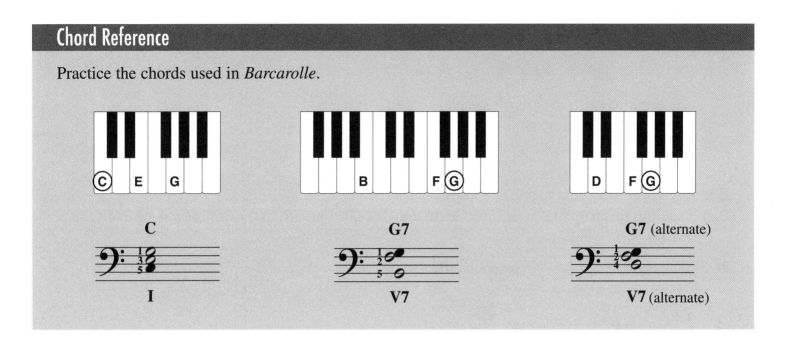

Rocking-Chord Accompaniment

When you can comfortably play *Barcarolle* with **blocked chords**, practice playing the melody with this L.H. accompaniment pattern.

Example:

More Ledger Lines

Review

Ledger lines are used to extend the staff.
The pieces in this unit explore *upper, inner,* and *lower* ledger notes.

Reading Hint: The letter names **A-C-E** are each a 3rd apart.
Remembering this pattern can help you learn the UPPER, INNER, and LOWER ledger line notes.

■ Play these exercises on the piano. Notice that *measure 1* skips and *measure 2* steps.

1. Upper Ledger Notes

2. Inner Ledger Notes

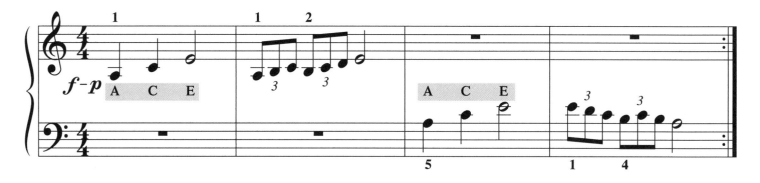

3. Lower Ledger Notes

pianoadventures.com/adult

Tchaikovsky wrote this dignified march as a memorial for soldiers of war.

March Slav

Peter Ilyich Tchaikovsky
(1840–1893, Russia)
arranged

DISCOVERY

The form of this arrangement is **A A¹**.
Name the two bass ledger notes used in **A¹**.

The opening of the Erie Canal in 1825 (connecting Lake Erie and the Hudson River) drew tens of thousands of settlers from the east to Detroit and made New York the country's primary financial center. The Canal trafficked lumber, produce, and manufactured goods hauled by barge and mule. *The Erie Canal* emerged as a folk song that celebrates this achievement in transportation.

The Erie Canal

Key of ____ Major/Minor

Traditional American

pianoadventures.com/adult

hauled some barg - es in our day___ filled with lum - ber,

coal, and hay.___ And we know ev - 'ry inch (of) the way,___

swing the 8ths!

all the way from Al - ba - ny to Buf - fa - lo!___

The form of this song is **Intro A A B A¹**. Label each section in the music.
Notice the **B section** opens in the relative major key (F major).

Duet: (Student plays *as written*)

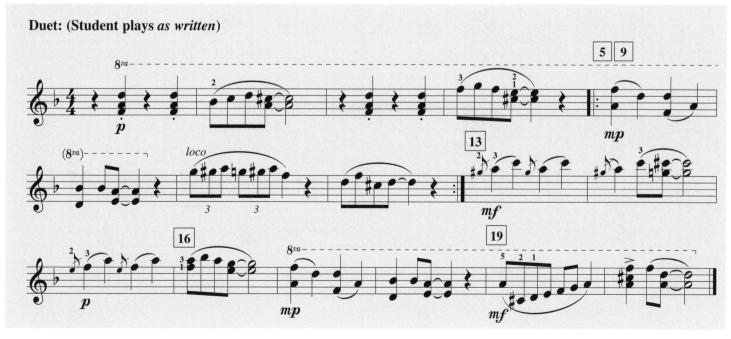

Edvard Grieg wrote the music for the play *Peer Gynt*, a colorful folk tale about the adventuresome travels of a Norwegian mountain boy. *Morning* was written for Act IV, when the young Peer Gynt has just arrived in Africa.

Morning
(from *Peer Gynt Suite No. 1*)

Key of ____ Major/Minor

Edvard Grieg
(1843–1907, Norway)
arranged

■ Notice the treble clef for the L.H. in *measures 33–40*.

Moderately slow

pianoadventures.com/adult

Technique Hints

▪ Drop with arm weight on the downbeat of each measure (L.H. finger 4).

▪ Play the R.H. thumb lightly for a smooth, *legato* sound.
  Play each scale as one continuous gesture between the hands.

Ascending Scales

Quickly, but steadily

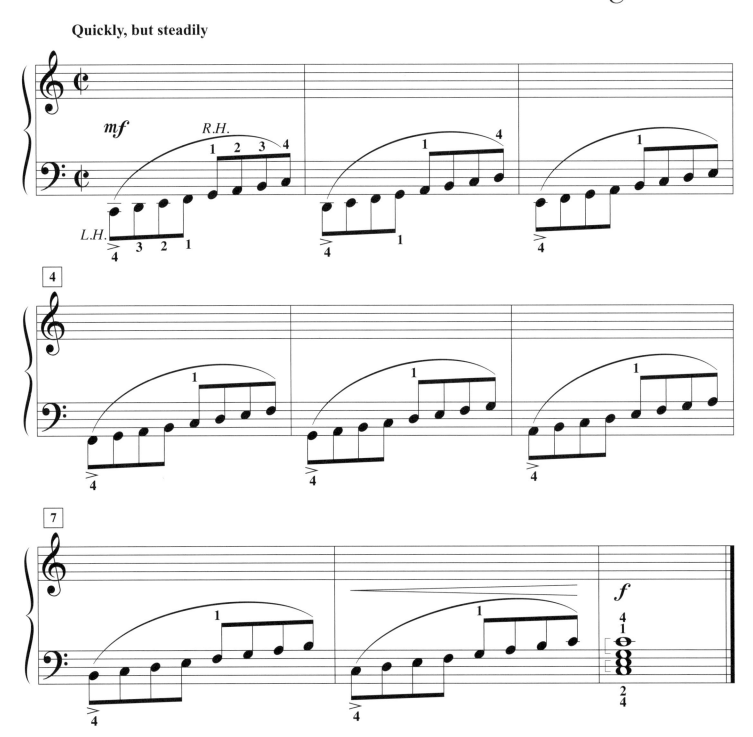

▪ Repeat *Ascending Scales* using swing rhythm.

pianoadventures.com/adult

Technique Hints

■ Drop with arm weight on the downbeat of each measure (R.H. finger 4).

■ Play the L.H. thumb lightly for a smooth, *legato* sound.
Play each scale as one continuous gesture between the hands.

Descending Scales

Quickly, but steadily

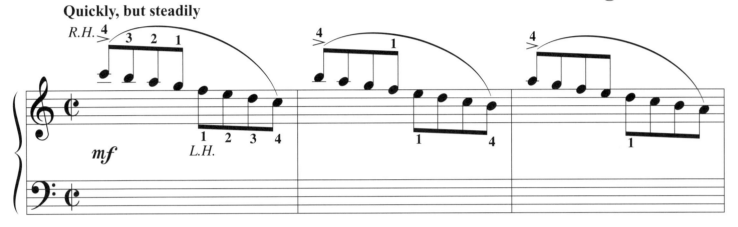

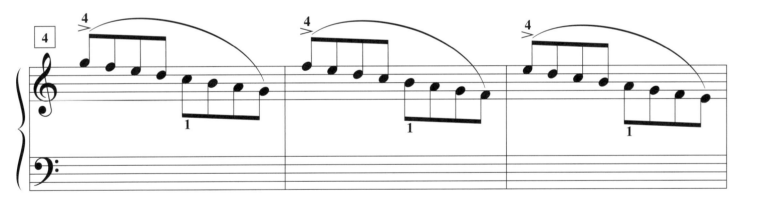

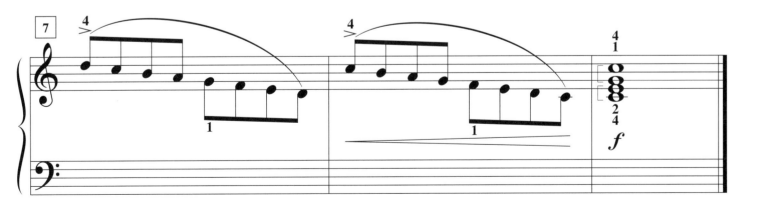

■ Repeat *Descending Scales* using swing rhythm.

The Glow Worm is an adaptation of a 1902 song from the German operetta *Lysistrata*. It has been featured in a Broadway musical and was recorded by both the Mills Brothers and Spike Jones, and the City Slickers during the 1940s and '50s.

Directions

■ First, play the melody alone for practice in reading *upper ledger line* notes.

■ Then add L.H. **blocked chords** on *beat 1* of each measure, as indicated by the chord symbols.

The Glow Worm

Lead Sheet

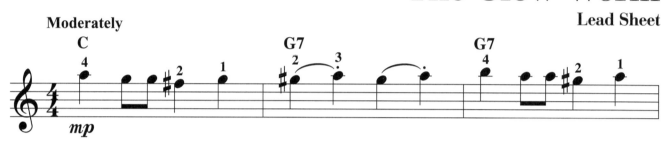

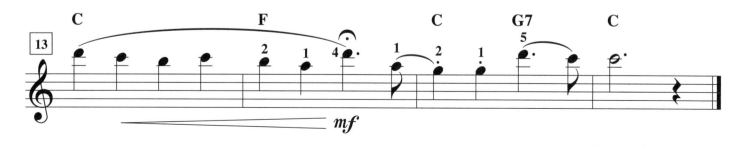

pianoadventures.com/adult

Half-Note Broken Chord Pattern

When you can comfortably play *The Glow Worm* with **blocked chords**, practice playing the melody with these two **broken-chord** accompaniment patterns.

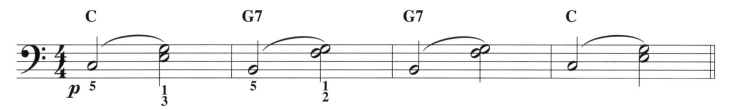

Example:

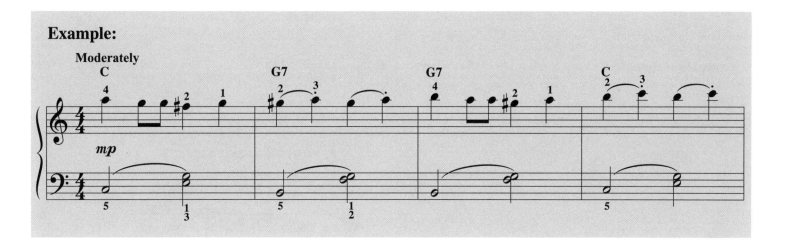

Quarter-Note Broken Chord Pattern

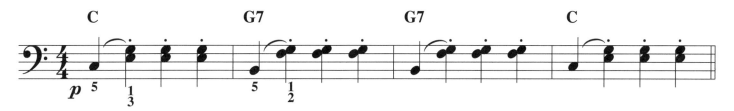

Example:

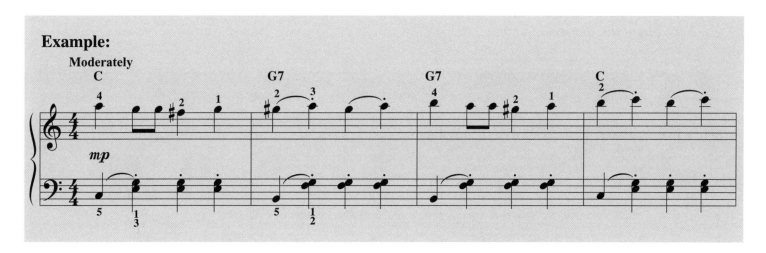

Key of E Minor

G Major and E Minor

Review: The **relative minor** scale begins on *scale degree 6* of the major scale.

New: The key of **E minor** is the RELATIVE MINOR of **G major**. (E is the 6th scale degree in the G major scale.) **E minor** and **G major** share the same key signature: one sharp (F♯).

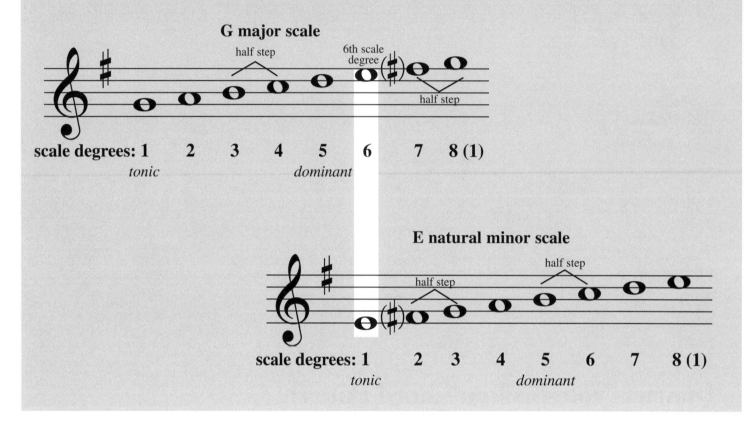

Playing and Listening

■ Play the **G major scale** and listen to the sound.
The major scale has **half steps** between *scale degrees 3–4* and *7–8*.

■ Now play the **E natural minor scale** (the relative minor scale).
Listen to the difference in sound. The natural minor scale has half steps between *scale degrees 2–3* and *5–6*.

Reminder

You can also find the **relative minor key** by counting down 3 half steps from the *tonic* of the major key.

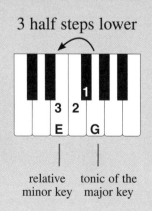

3 half steps lower

relative   tonic of the
minor key   major key

pianoadventures.com/adult

The **E NATURAL MINOR scale** shares the same key signature as the **G major scale**.

◼ Notice the **whole step** between scale *degrees* 7 and 8 in the natural minor scale.

◼ Practice hands separately, then hands together.

E Natural Minor Scale

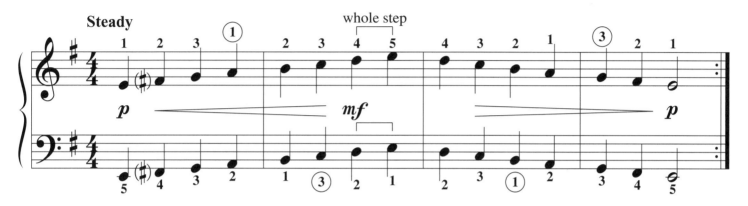

For the HARMONIC MINOR scale, raise the 7th scale degree a half step.

This forms a **half step** between *scale degrees 7* and *8* (leading tone to tonic).
Remember, an accidental is needed to raise the 7th scale degree.

E harmonic minor scale

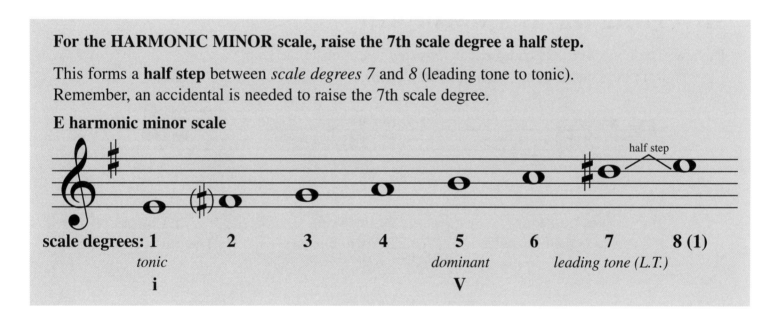

scale degrees: 1	2	3	4	5	6	7	8 (1)
tonic				*dominant*		*leading tone (L.T.)*	
i				**V**			

◼ Practice hands separately, then hands together.

E Harmonic Minor Scale

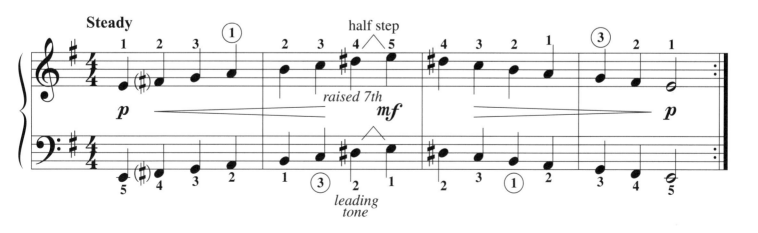

Primary Chords in E Minor: i - iv - V7

Review: In a minor key, the **i** and **iv** chords are minor.
The **V** chord is usually major.

■ Find and play the ROOT POSITION primary chords in the **Key of E minor** shown below.

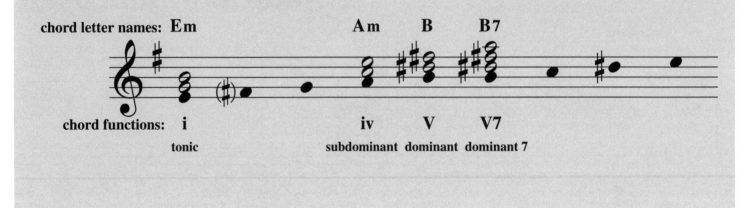

Inverting the iv Chord: Am

Review: The notes of the **iv** chord can be *inverted* to eliminate the leap
   from the **i** chord to the **iv** chord (**Em** to **Am**).

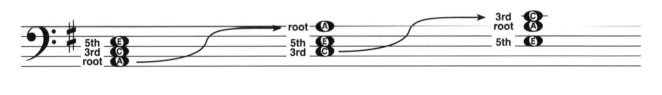

root position	**1st inversion**	**2nd inversion**
The root is the bass note.	The 3rd is in the bass. (The root, A, moves up an octave)	The 5th is in the bass.

E Minor: i-iv Chords in Close Position

The **2nd inversion** of the **iv chord** (Am) is often used to play **i-iv** chords in *close position*.

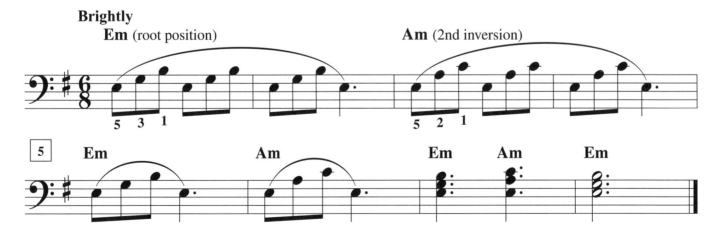

The V7 Chord in E Minor: B7

The **B7 chord** is a four-note chord built up in **3rds** from **B**.

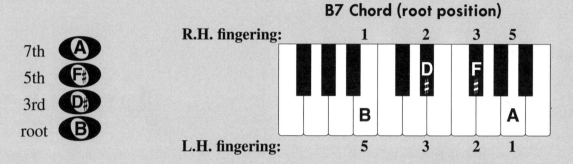

7th Ⓐ
5th Ⓕ#
3rd Ⓓ#
root Ⓑ

B7 Chord (root position)

R.H. fingering:

L.H. fingering:

B is *scale degree 5* (the dominant) in the Key of E minor.
The **B7** chord is the **V7** or **dominant 7th** chord in the Key of E minor.

Inverting the V7 Chord: B7

An inversion of the **B7** chord eliminates the leap between root position chords.

root position The root is the bass note.	**root position** with the 5th omitted (a 3-note B7 chord)	**1st inversion** The 3rd is in the bass. (the 5th is omitted)	**2nd inversion** The 5th is in the bass. (the 3rd is omitted)

E Minor: i-iv-V7 Chords in Close Position

An inversion of the **V7** chord (B7) allows the **i-iv-V7** chords to be played in *close position*.

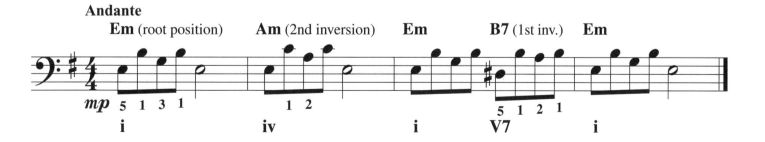

Tenuto Mark (stress mark) 𝅘𝅥

This mark means to hold the note its full value.
Hint: Press deeply into the key.

Musical Form Check

◼ Label the sections of this piece.

◼ Name the form: _____

Lunar Eclipse

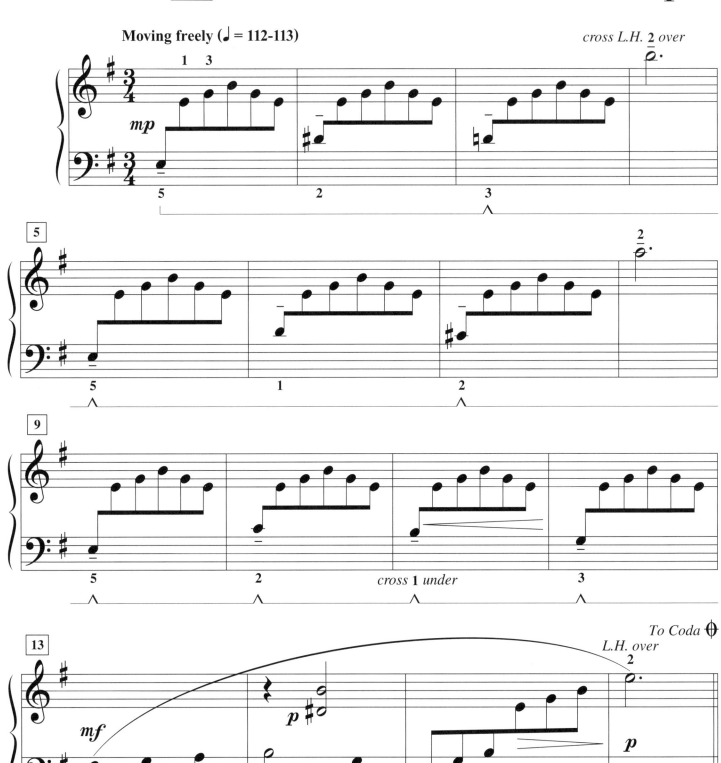

🔊 pianoadventures.com/adult

■ In *measures 17–20* the R.H. plays both the melody and harmony (two voices).
Play the upper voice **mf** with a rich tone. Play the thumb *lightly* for the inner voice.

 DISCOVERY   Circle three different **7ths** in this piece.

- Create an expressive R.H. melody by shaping with ⎯⎯◁ and ▷⎯⎯ marks.

- Play the L.H. chords more softly, staying close to the keys.

Swan Lake
Theme from *Overture to Act II*
Key of ____ Major/Minor

Peter Ilyich Tchaikovsky
(1840–1893, Russia)
arranged

Find an example of these chords: **E minor** (root position)   **D major** (root position)

A minor (2nd inversion)   **C major** (1st inversion)

Scale Warm-up

■ Let your thumb follow behind each finger being played.

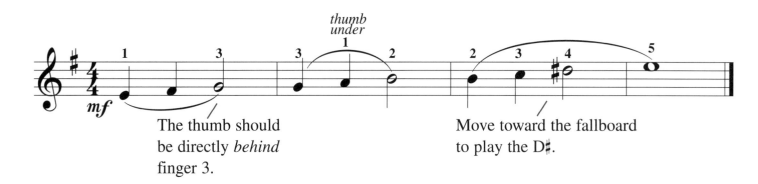

The thumb should
be directly *behind*
finger 3.

Move toward the fallboard
to play the D♯.

E Minor Scale Study
(with i, iv, and V7 chords)

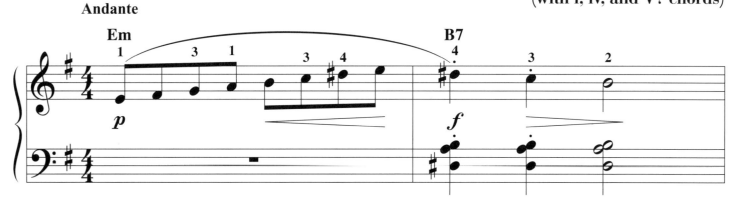

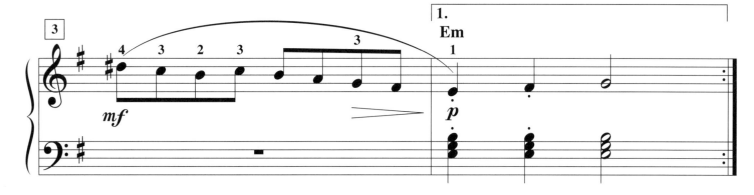

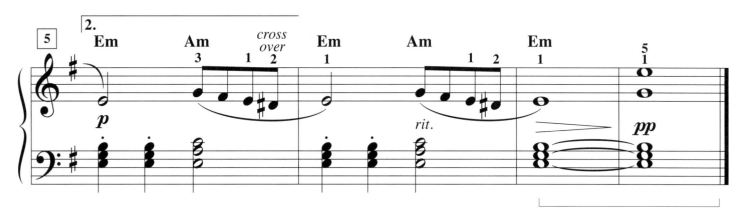

pianoadventures.com/adult

Technique Hints

■ First, play each broken chord as a **blocked chord**. Then play as written. Listen for smooth, *legato* crossings between the hands.

■ Observe all **dynamic marks**. For a deep, rich tone, use *more* weight; for a softer tone, use *less* weight.

E Minor
Arpeggio Study

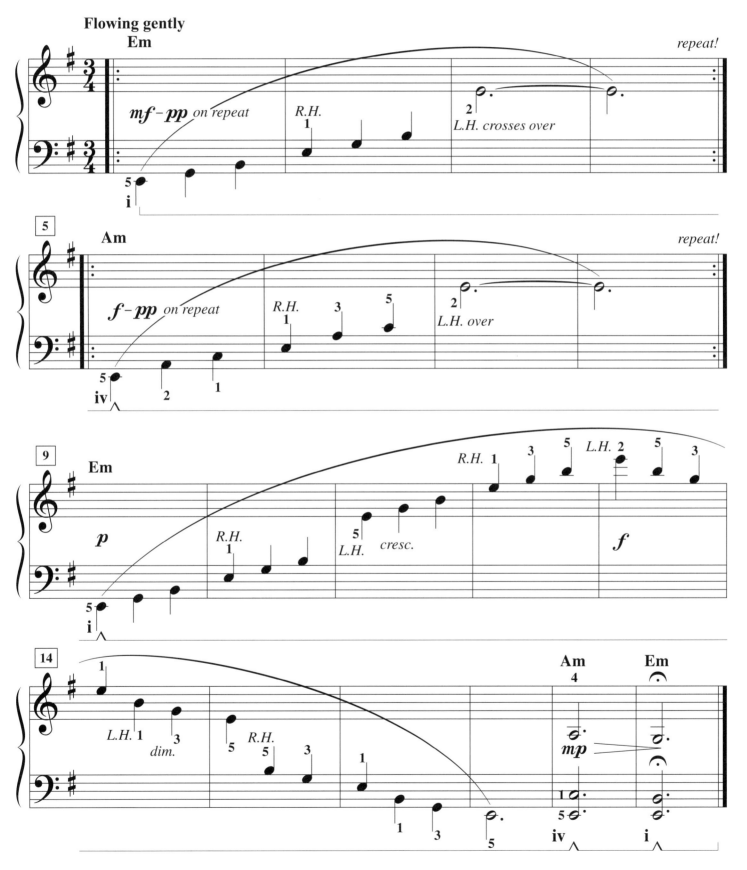

■ Transpose this study to the keys of **A minor** and **D minor**.

> *House of the Rising Sun* has traditional American roots and has been popularized by both folk and rock musicians, including Bob Dylan. The Animals made it a hit in 1964 with the "agonized delivery" of Eric Burdon and the sparse keyboard style of Alan Price on the Vox Continental electronic organ.

Directions

■ First, play the melody alone with pedal.

■ Then add L.H. **blocked chords** on *beat 1* of each measure, as indicated by the chord symbols.

Play all of the chords in **root position**, except the **B7** chord, which may be played in 1st inversion (for close position).

House of the Rising Sun

E Minor Lead Sheet

Traditional

pianoadventures.com/adult

¾ Broken-Chord Pattern (♩ ♩)

When you can comfortably play *House of the Rising Sun* with **blocked chords**, practice playing the melody with these L.H. accompaniment patterns.

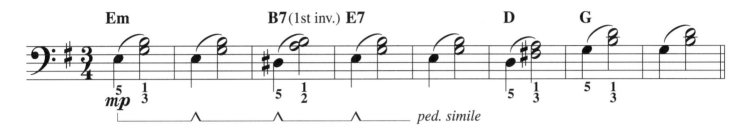

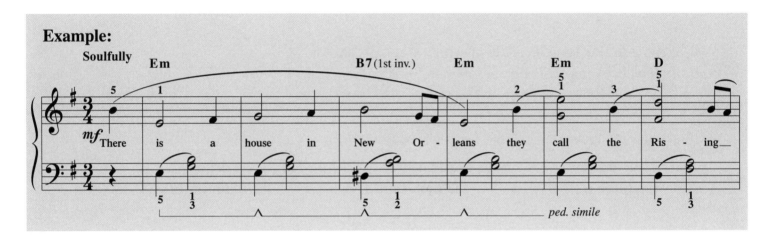

¾ Broken-Chord Pattern (♫ ♩)

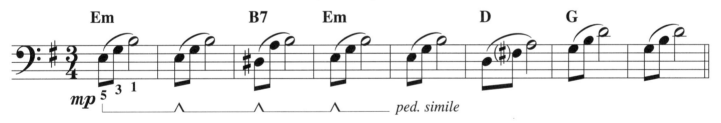

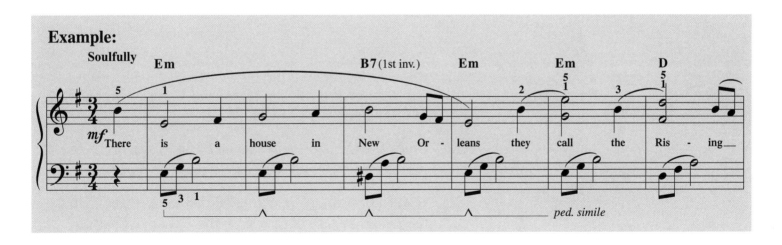

Key of D Major

The D Major Scale

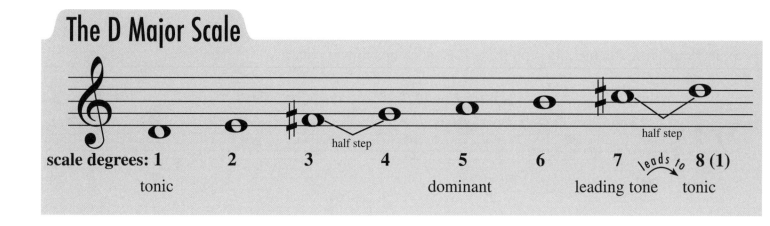

scale degrees: **1**   **2**   **3**   **4**   **5**   **6**   **7** *leads to* **8 (1)**

tonic   dominant   leading tone   tonic

half step

half step

Review: a **major scale** is made of **whole steps** except for
half steps between *scale degrees 3–4* and *7–8*.

Find and play these tones in the Key of D Major:

- Scale degree 1,
  the **tonic (D)**.
- Scale degree 5,
  the **dominant (A)**.
- Scale degree 7,
  the **leading tone (C♯)**.

Listen and Discover

- Using R.H. finger 3, play the **D major scale** and stop on the *leading tone*.
  Do you hear how the *leading tone* pulls up to the *tonic* note D?

- Complete the scale by playing the *tonic*.

Key Signature for D Major

The half step between *scale degrees 3–4* and *7–8*
requires the **F** (scale degree 3) and **C** (scale degree 7)
to be sharped (**F♯** and **C♯**).

Since the D major scale has an F♯ and C♯, a piece in
the **Key of D Major** will use F♯ and C♯ throughout.

Instead of a sharp appearing before every F and C in
the piece, a sharp is shown on the *F line* and *C space*
at the beginning of each staff.

pianoadventures.com/adult

<table>
<tr>
<td>

Parallel Motion

Notes moving in the same direction.

</td>
<td>

Contrary Motion

Notes moving in opposite directions.

</td>
</tr>
</table>

D Major Scale in Parallel Motion

■ Practice hands separately, then hands together.

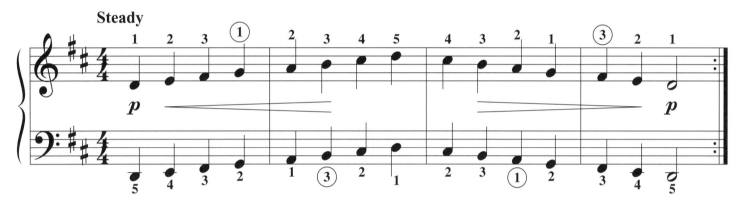

D Major Scale in Contrary Motion

■ Notice that the *same* fingers play *together* for **contrary motion**.

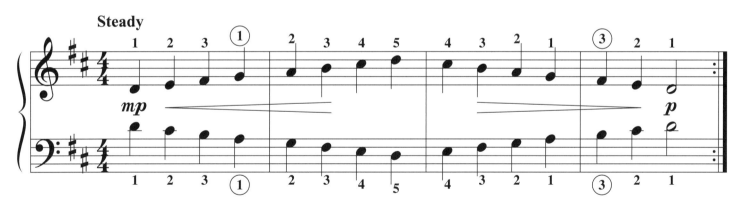

Metronome Practice

Put a ✓ in the blank when you can play the D major scale **hands alone** at these tempi.
Play each hand *ascending*, then *descending*.

legato ♩ = 88 ___	*legato* ♩ = 112 ___	*legato* ♩ = 144 ___
staccato ♩ = 88 ___	*staccato* ♩ = 112 ___	*staccato* ♩ = 144 ___

■ Find and play the ROOT POSITION primary chords in the **Key of D** shown below.

Inverting the IV Chord: G

Review: The notes of the **IV** chord can be *inverted* to eliminate the leap
from the **I** chord to the **IV** chord (**D** to **G**).

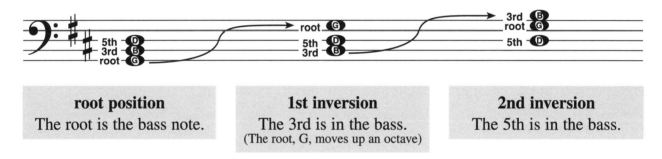

root position	**1st inversion**	**2nd inversion**
The root is the bass note.	The 3rd is in the bass. (The root, G, moves up an octave)	The 5th is in the bass.

D Major: I-IV Chords in Close Position

The **2nd inversion** of the **IV chord** (G) is often used to play **I-IV** chords in *close position*.

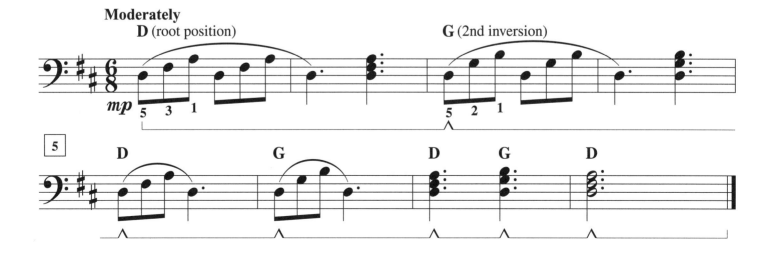

The V7 Chord in D Major: A7

The **A7 chord** is a four-note chord built up in **3rds** from **A**.

Review: When A (the root) is the *lowest* note, the chord is in ROOT POSITION.

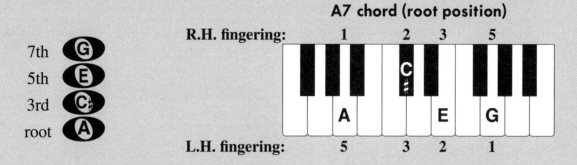

7th **G**
5th **E**
3rd **C♯**
root **A**

A7 chord (root position)

R.H. fingering: 1 2 3 5

L.H. fingering: 5 3 2 1

A is *scale degree 5* (the dominant) in the Key of D major.
The **A7** chord is the **V7** or **dominant 7th** chord in the Key of D major.

Inverting the V7 Chord: A7

An inversion of the **A7** chord eliminates the leap between root position chords.

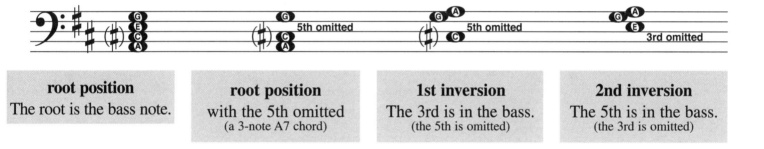

root position	**root position**	**1st inversion**	**2nd inversion**
The root is the bass note.	with the 5th omitted (a 3-note A7 chord)	The 3rd is in the bass. (the 5th is omitted)	The 5th is in the bass. (the 3rd is omitted)

D Major: I-IV-V7 Chords in Close Position

An inversion of the **V7** chord (A7) allows the **I-IV-V7** chords to be played in *close position*.

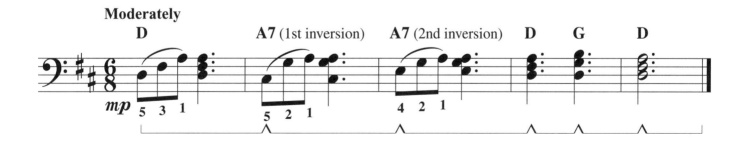

This theme from the last movement of Beethoven's ninth symphony is one of the most famous melodies of all time. The theme is introduced softly by the string basses and is later played *forte* by full orchestra and chorus, for a victorious ending. Beethoven wrote and conducted his ninth symphony when he was completely deaf. When the audience broke into thunderous applause, a friend had to turn Beethoven around so he would see the overwhelming response to his final symphony.

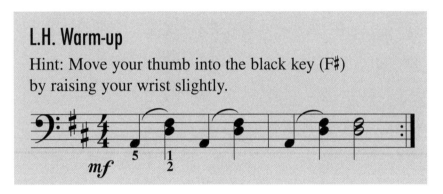

L.H. Warm-up

Hint: Move your thumb into the black key (F#) by raising your wrist slightly.

Song of Joy

Theme from *Symphony No. 9*

Key of ____ Major

Ludwig van Beethoven
(1770–1827)
arranged

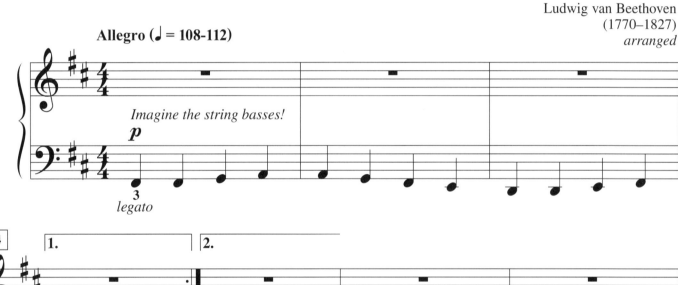

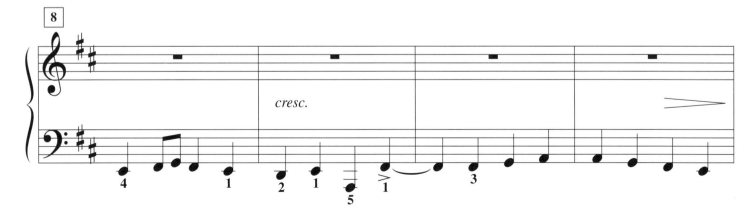

 DISCOVERY The opening L.H. melody begins on *scale degree 3* (F-sharp in the Key of D major).
Transpose *Song of Joy* down a whole step to the **Key of C major**.

Practice Suggestions

- Practice hands alone. Notice the patterns.

- Next, s-l-o-w-l-y play hands together. You will find some measures more difficult than others.

- Isolate the tricky measures and practice them repeatedly 3–8 times.

- Gradually play up to tempo.

Gavotte in D Major

James Hook
(1746–1827, England)
original form (transposed from C major)

pianoadventures.com/adult

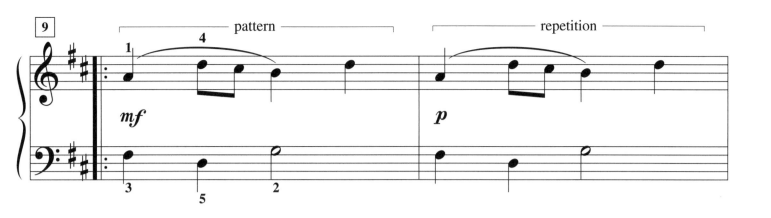

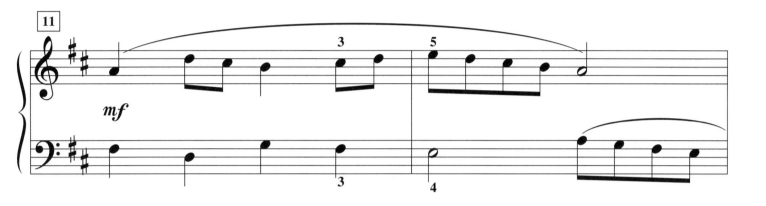

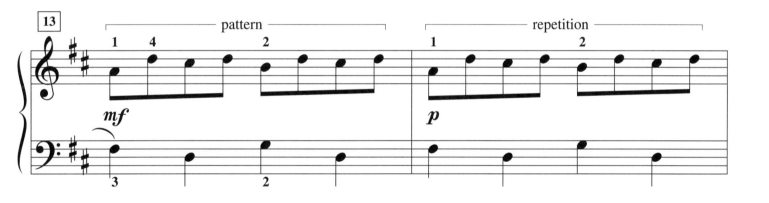

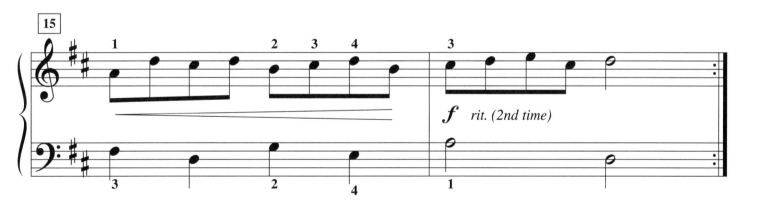

What is the form of this piece: binary or ternary?
Transpose this piece to **C major**.

A scale often *leads* to a particular note.

◼ Before playing this piece, circle the note that is the "goal" for each scale.

◼ Listen for **musical direction** in your playing.

◼ Practice at **slow**, **medium**, and **fast** tempi.

Scale Study in D Major

Ferdinand Beyer
Op. 101, Tonlieder in D
original form

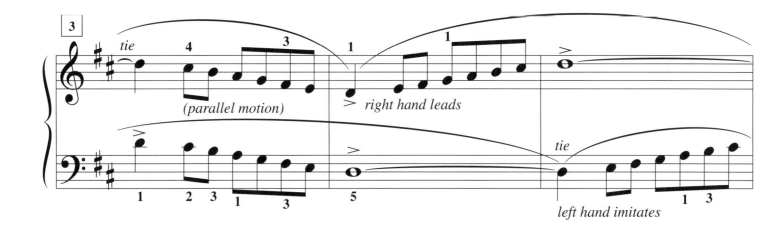

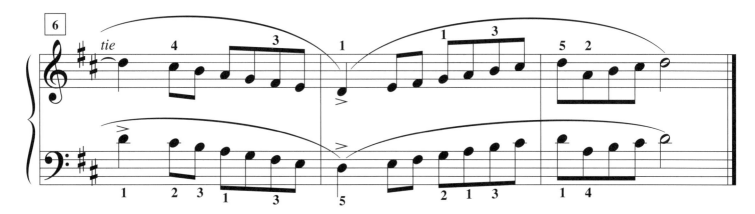

◼ Transpose to the keys of **C major** and **G major**.

pianoadventures.com/adult

Technique Hints

- Begin the L.H. *crossover* while the R.H. is playing.

- Extend (open) the L.H. to easily play the octaves in *measures 3–4, 7–8,* and *15–16.*

Chord Study in D Major

Worried Man Blues is an old chain-gang tune. It was reworked in the late '50s by The Kingston Trio to tell the story of a man whose only worry in life is whether his girlfriend Sue is faithful while he is traveling on a business trip.

Directions

◼ First, play the melody alone with pedal.

◼ Then play **root position blocked 5ths** on *beat 1* of each measure, as indicated by the chord symbol.

Worried Man Blues
D Major Lead Sheet

Traditional

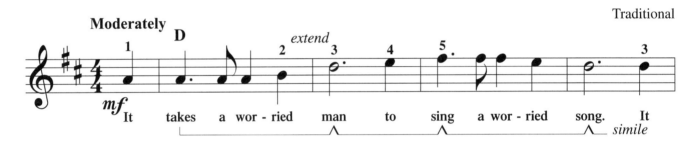

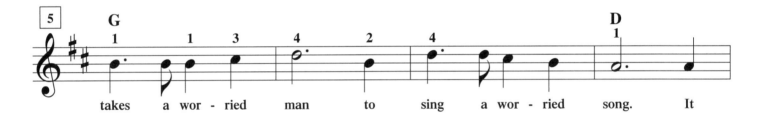

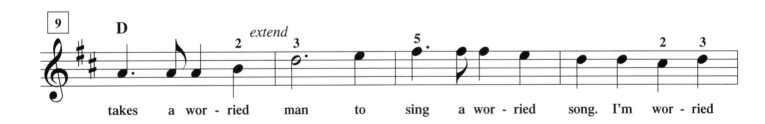

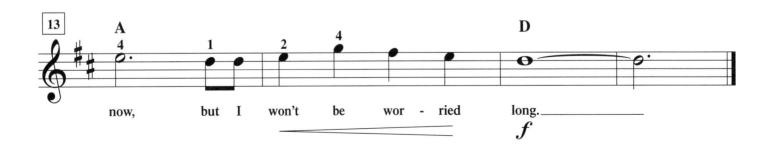

pianoadventures.com/adult

5th-6th Accompaniment Pattern (♩ ♩)

When you can comfortably play the melody for *Worried Man Blues* with **blocked 5ths**, try these two accompaniment patterns, which use a **5th-6th** pattern.

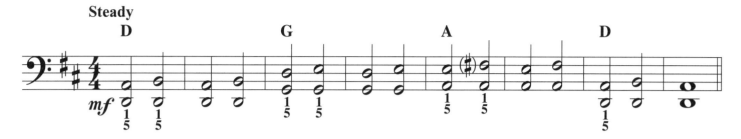

Example:

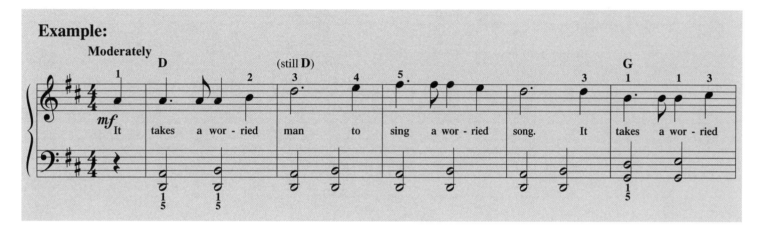

5th-6th Accompaniment Pattern (♩ ♩ ♩)

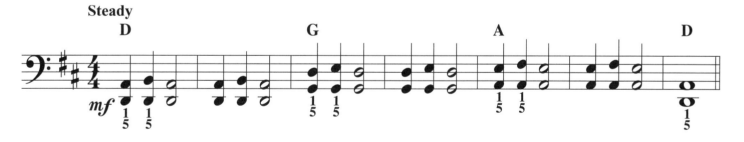

Example:

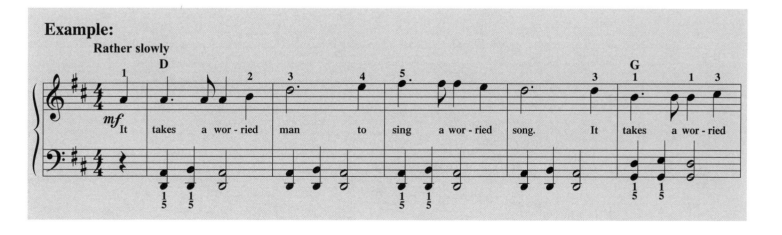

One-Octave Arpeggios

Review: *Arpeggio* means "harp-like."

To play a **one-octave arpeggio**, the hand is *extended* over the keys.

■ Practice these arpeggios slowly with a loose, relaxed wrist. Notice the R.H. fingering is **1-2-3-5**.

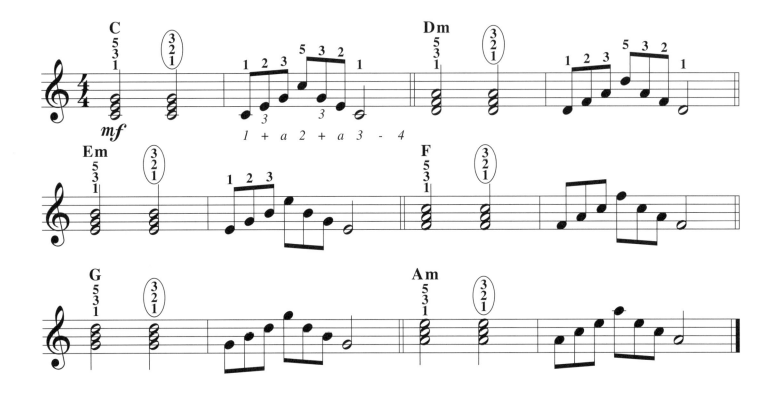

■ Now play L.H. one-octave arpeggios. Notice the fingering is **5-4-2-1**.

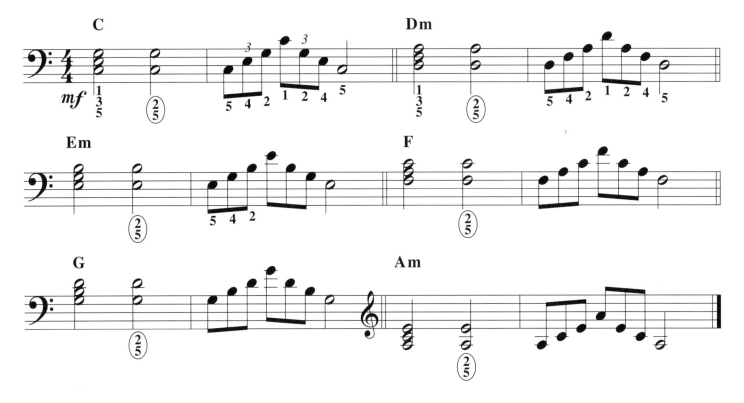

pianoadventures.com/adult

Mozart's *Eine Kleine Nachtmusik* (A Little Night Music) was originally written for a string quintet. Here is the opening theme, which demands precise rhythm.

Theme from
Eine Kleine Nachtmusik

Wolfgang Amadeus Mozart
(1756–1791, Austria)
arranged

■ First practice *measures 1–4* hands alone, then hands together.

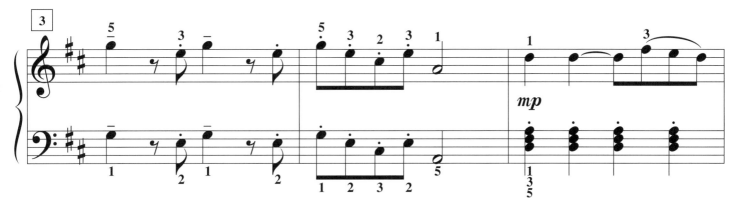

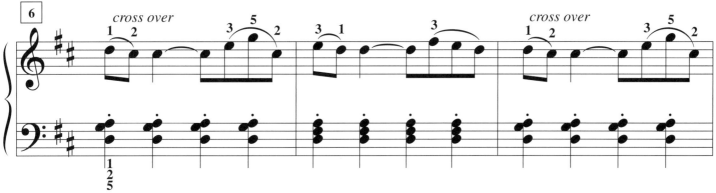

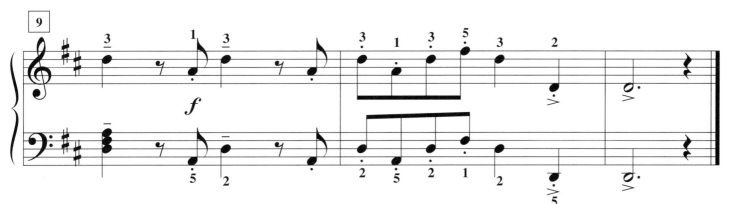

What chord is outlined in *measures 1–2?* _____
What chord is outlined in *measures 3–4?* _____

Dynamic Mark

$f\!f$ – *fortissimo*

Fortissimo means very loud, louder than *forte* (f).

Mendelssohn composed the music for Shakespeare's play *A Midsummer Night's Dream* at the request of King Frederick William. The *Wedding March* appears at the end of the play for a triple wedding ceremony.

Wedding March
from *A Midsummer Night's Dream*

Felix Mendelssohn
(1809–1847, Germany)
arranged

Bright March tempo (♩ = 120-132)

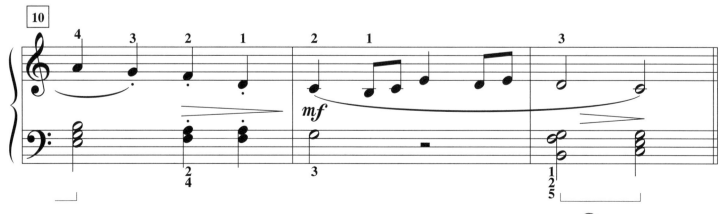

pianoadventures.com/adult

DISCOVERY   Label the sections in the music: **Intro A B A Coda**

Review: Syncopation

Syncopation occurs when notes are accented
BETWEEN the beats instead of ON the beat.

■ Play this example, counting aloud.

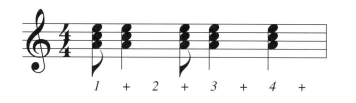

1 + 2 + 3 + 4 +

Fiesta España

Nancy Faber

pianoadventures.com/adult

DISCOVERY The harmony of this piece is based on four triads.
Name them, indicating major or minor. ____, ____, ____, ____

One-Octave Arpeggio Hint

■ To play a one-octave arpeggio for the R.H., use a circular "**under and over**" motion of the wrist.

The words are a guide for your arpeggio technique.

Arpeggio Power
(for R.H.)

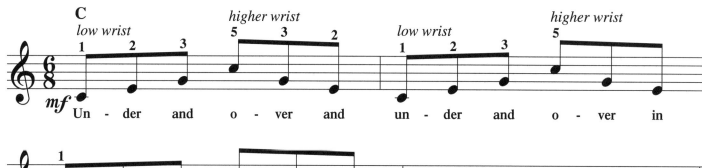

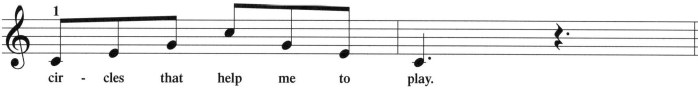

Continue playing R.H. arpeggios on F, G, and Am chords.

pianoadventures.com/adult

One-Octave Arpeggio Hint

■ To play a one-octave arpeggio for the L.H., use a circular "**under and over**" motion of the wrist.

Notice this motion is the mirror image of the R.H.

Arpeggio Power
(for L.H.)

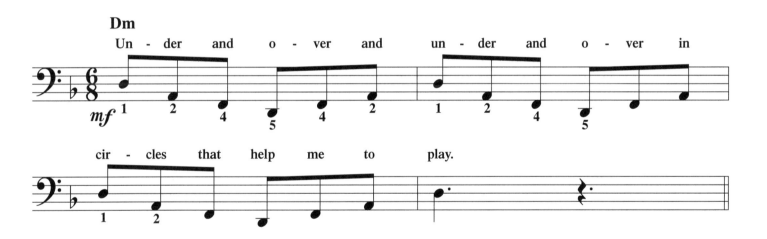

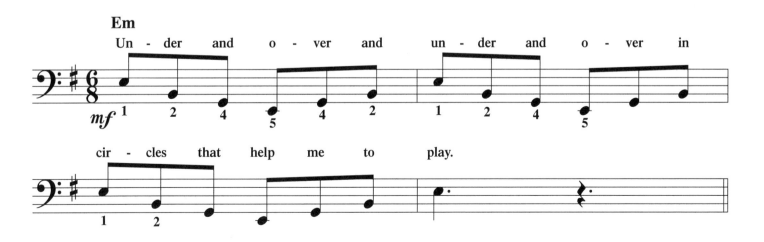

Continue playing L.H. arpeggios on F, G, and Am chords.

> Franz Liszt was the most esteemed pianist of the Romantic Period
> and *Liebestraum* is one of his best-loved works. When pianist
> Vladimir Horowitz played Liszt's *Liebestraum* during his historic
> "return to Moscow concert" in 1986, many were moved to tears.
> The concert was televised for all the world to see.

Directions

◼ First, play the melody alone with pedal.

◼ Then add L.H. root position **blocked chords** on *beat 1*
of each measure, as indicated by the chord symbols.

Liebestraum
(Dream of Love)
Key of _____ Major/Minor

Franz Liszt
(1811–1886, Hungary)

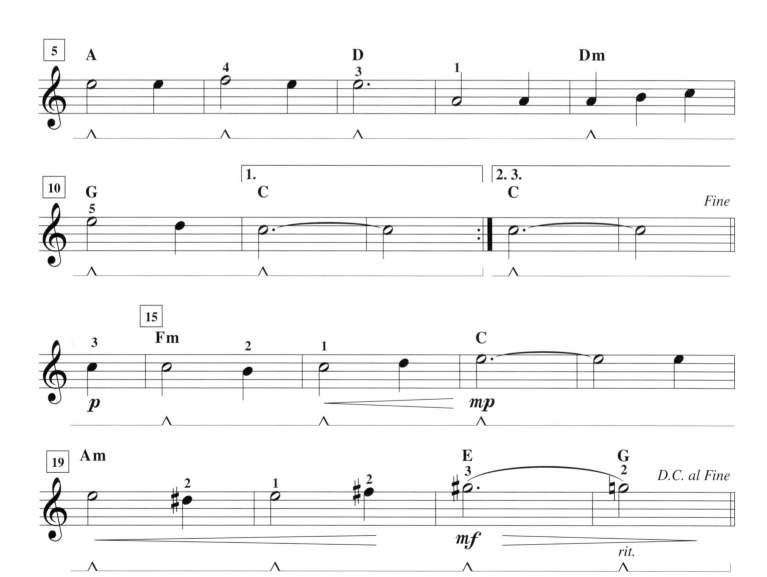

pianoadventures.com/adult

Arpeggio Accompaniment

■ First, practice this L.H. accompaniment, listening for smooth chord changes.

■ When you can easily play the one-octave arpeggios, use this pattern to accompany *Liebestraum*.

Example:

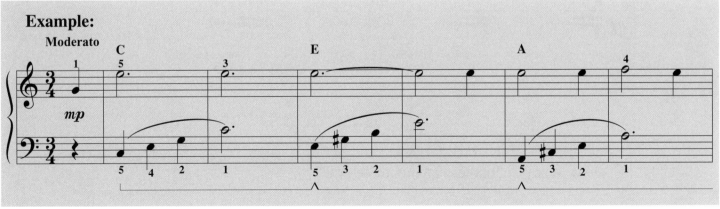

Sixteenth Notes

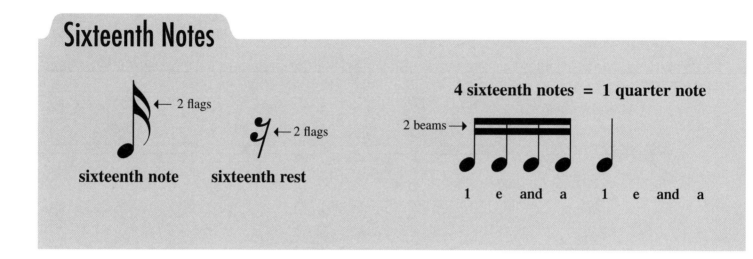

Sixteenth Notes

sixteenth note ← 2 flags

sixteenth rest ← 2 flags

4 sixteenth notes = 1 quarter note

2 beams →

1 e and a 1 e and a

Feeling the Rhythm

■ Tap (or clap) the rhythms below. Then play and transpose to other keys.

1.

mf

Count: 1 e + a 2 e + a 3 e + a 4 (e) + (a)

Am - a - de - us Mo-zart

■ This rhythm should have the same *feel* as saying "Bugs Bun-ny."

2.

mf 5 3 1 5

1 (e) + a 2 (e) + a 3 (e) + a 4 (e + a)

Bugs Bun - ny

■ This rhythm should have the same *feel* as saying "Car-y Grant."

3.

mf 5 3 1 5

1 e + (a) 2 e + (a) 3 e + (a) 4 e + (a)

Car - y Grant

DISCOVERY How many 16th notes equal one 8th note? _____

pianoadventures.com/adult

Drummer at the Keyboard

■ On the closed key cover, tap your R.H. and L.H. together as you count aloud.
Practice this exercise until you can do it with ease. Can you tap with the metronome at ♩ = 69?

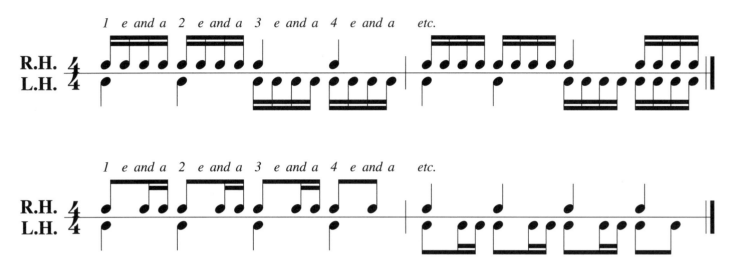

■ Practice this rhythm warm-up as written.
Then transpose to the keys suggested.

Rhythm Warm-up

Lively, with precise rhythm (♩ = 72-88)

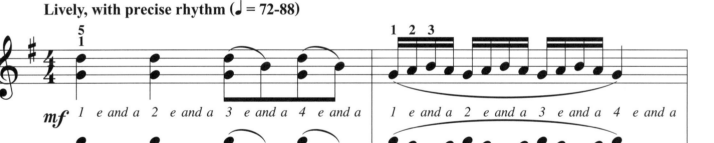

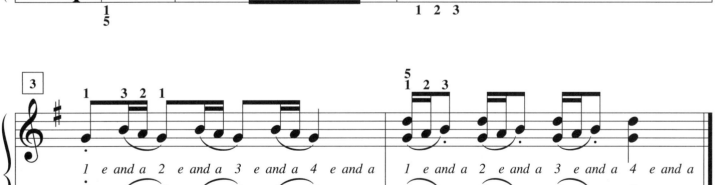

DISCOVERY Transpose *Rhythm Warm-up* to these keys: G minor, D major, and D minor.

Notice the *theme* is mostly eighth notes.

Variations 1 and *2* use the ♫♫♪ rhythm.

■ Can you find the ♪♫♪ rhythm in *Variation 3*?

Sea Chantey

Key of ____ Major/Minor

Traditional melody

pianoadventures.com/adult

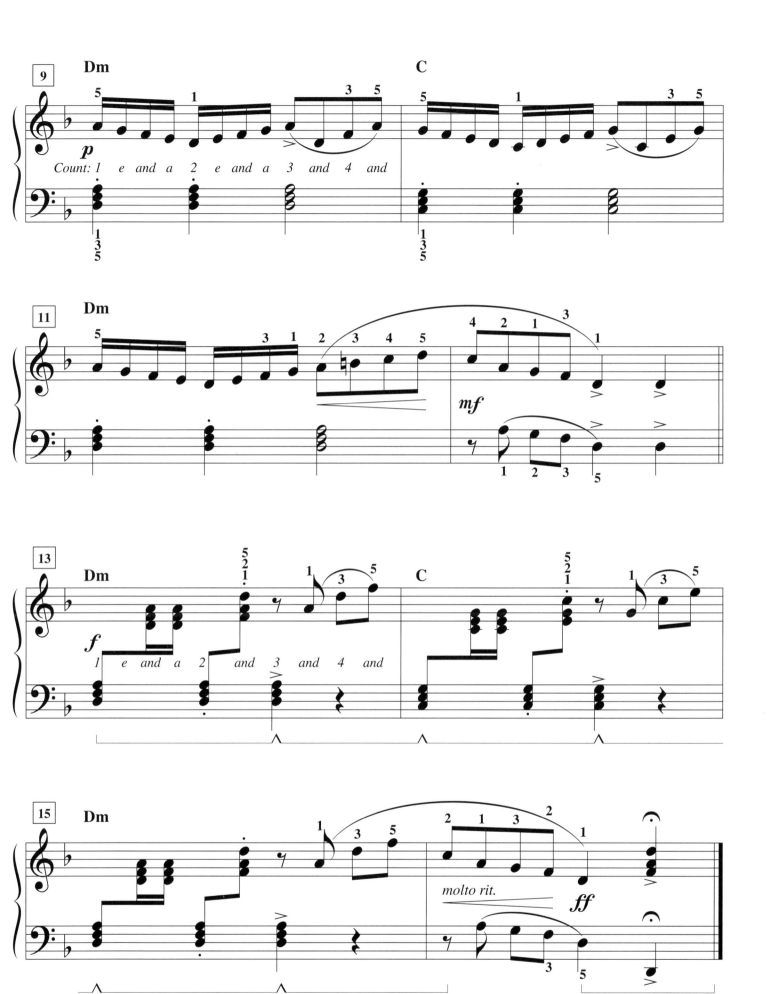

Count: 1 e and a 2 e and a 3 and 4 and

1 e and a 2 and 3 and 4 and

CREATIVE Explore playing your own variation of *Sea Chantey*.
(Hint: Change the rhythm, notes, dynamics, etc.)

Musetta's Waltz (*Quando me'n vo' soletta*) is a much loved aria from *La Bohème* (Act II) by Giacomo Puccini. Phenomenally successful from its debut in 1896, *La Bohème* continues to be one of the most beloved of the Italian operas.

Musetta's Waltz
from the opera *La Bohème*

Giacomo Puccini
(1858–1924, Italy)
arranged

pianoadventures.com/adult

DISCOVERY

In *measure 30*, the sixteenth notes begin on *beat 1*.
On which beat do the sixteenth notes occur in the rest of the piece? beat ____

Each line of music uses a different **sixteenth-note** rhythm pattern.

■ Practice each line of music hands alone, then hands together.

■ You may wish to practice these patterns using the metronome marks shown at the bottom of the page.

Rhythm Trainer
Sixteenth-Note Rhythm Study

Rhythm pattern: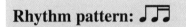

Rhythm pattern:

Rhythm pattern: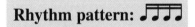

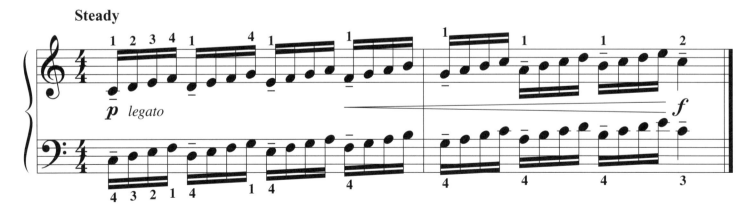

Andante ♩ = 69 ___   *Moderato* ♩ = 80 ___   *Allegro* ♩ = 92 ___

pianoadventures.com/adult

Technique Hints

■ Practice the R.H. alone, shaping each scale passage with a *cresc.* and *dim.*

■ Practice the L.H. alone, lifting gently for *beats 2* and *3*.

Scale Journey
Sixteenth-Note Scale Study

Though Borodin's profession as a medical doctor and researcher occupied most of his time, he nonetheless achieved lasting fame as a composer. The Russian composer dedicated his *Second String Quartet in D* to his wife, a concert pianist. The third movement *Nocturne*, which has been described as a "haunting love song without words," is luxuriant in texture. The famous melody is played by the cello—an instrument that Borodin himself played.

Directions

▪ First, play the melody alone with pedal.

▪ Then play L.H. **blocked 5ths** on *beat 1* of each measure, as indicated by the chord symbols.

Nocturne
from *String Quartet No. 2*

Alexander Borodin
(1833–1887, Russia)

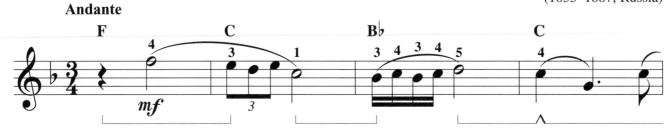

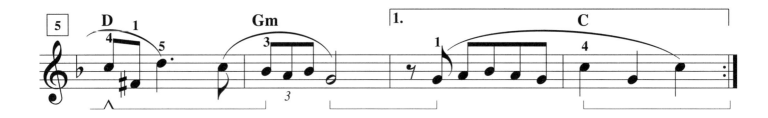

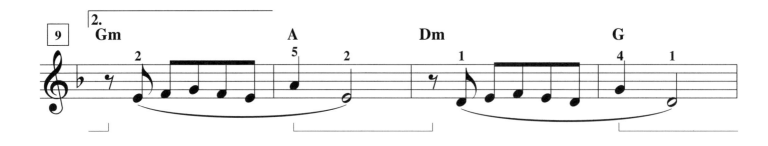

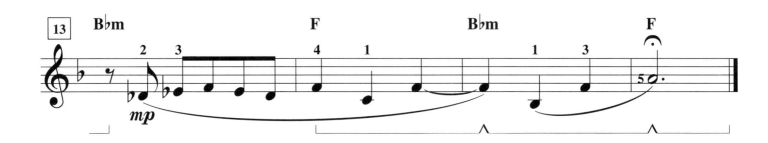

pianoadventures.com/adult

When you can comfortably play *Nocturne* with **blocked chords**,
practice using these L.H. accompaniment patterns.

Broken 5th Accompaniment

Example:

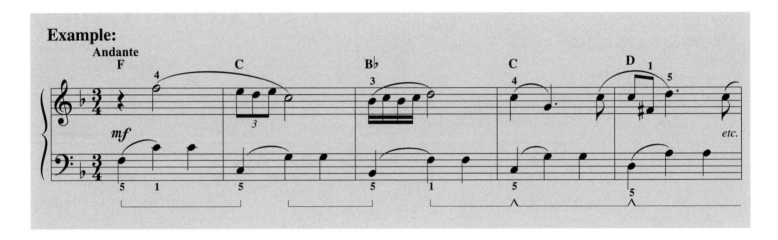

Root-5th-Octave Accompaniment

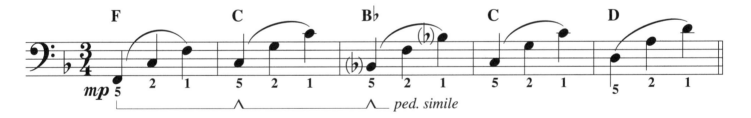

Example:

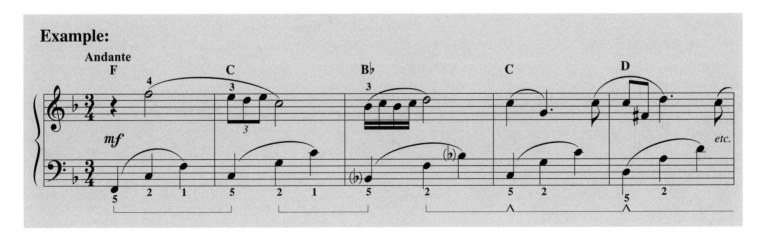

Review Piece

Pachelbel's *Canon* is one of the most popular pieces of all time.
It has been featured in movies, television, and in countless recordings and concerts.

The canon is based on this four-measure chord pattern which repeats throughout the piece:

chord names:	‖:	C	G	Am	Em	F	C	F	G	:‖
chord functions:	‖	I	V	vi	iii	IV	I	IV	V	‖

Pachelbel Canon

■ Write the chord letter names for *measures 1–4.*

Johann Pachelbel
(1653–1706, Germany)
arranged

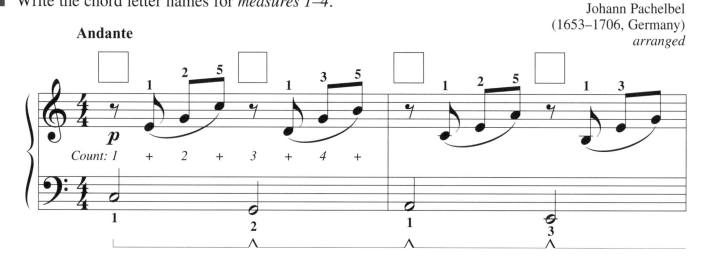

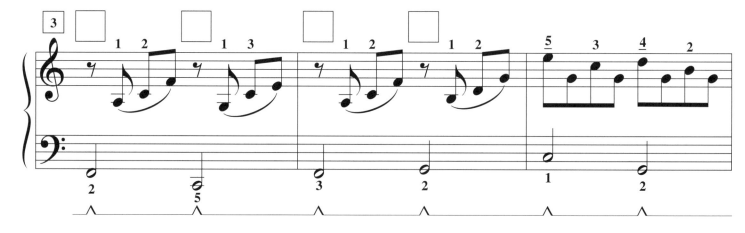

pianoadventures.com/adult

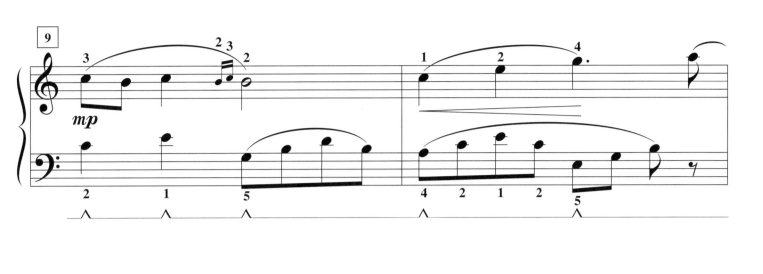

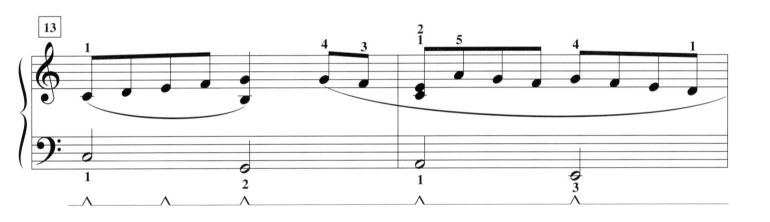

189

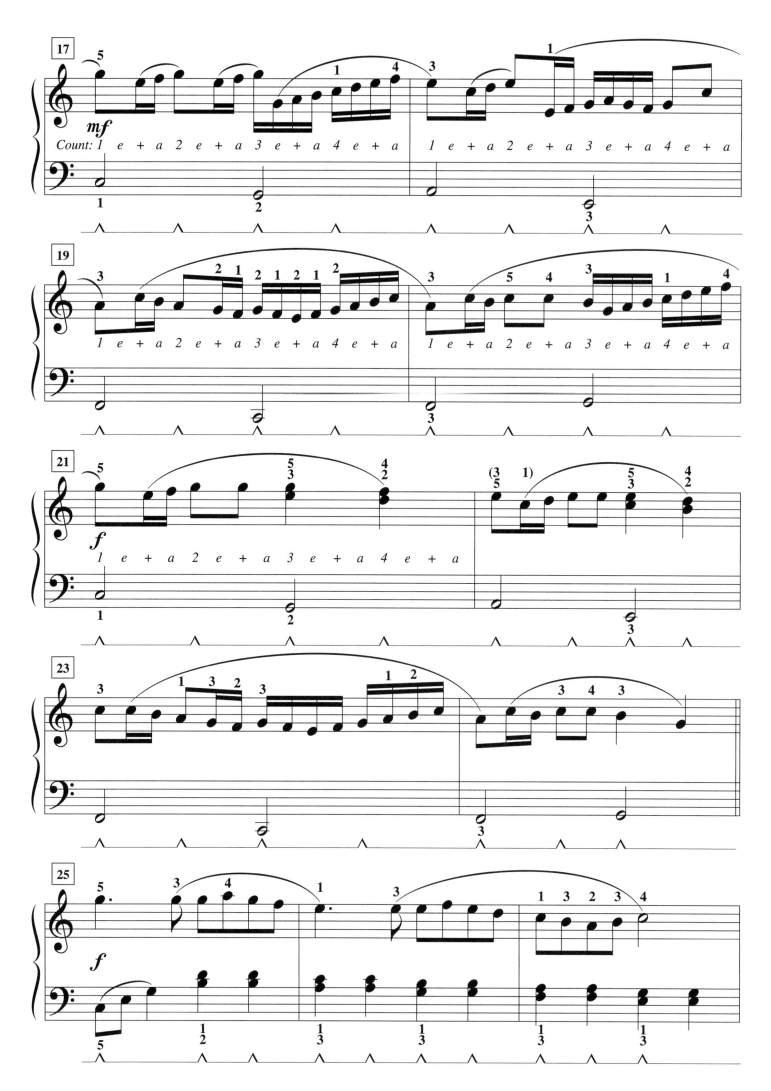

Find and listen to one of the many recordings of Pachelbel's *Canon in D*.
Listen for the repeating bass line, which supports the melodic variations.

Scale Chart

■ Practice these scales hands separately, then hands together.
Listen for the fingers playing *exactly* together.

■ Draw a ✓ in the blank when you can accurately play
at the metronome marks given.

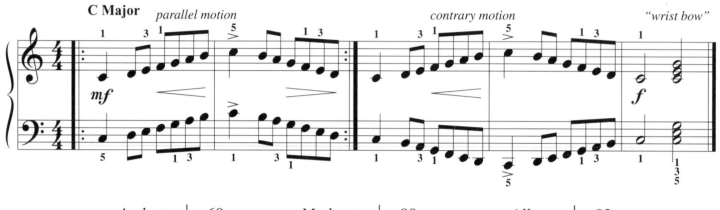

C Major   *parallel motion*   *contrary motion*   *"wrist bow"*

Andante ♩ = 69 ___   *Moderato* ♩ = 80 ___   *Allegro* ♩ = 92 ___

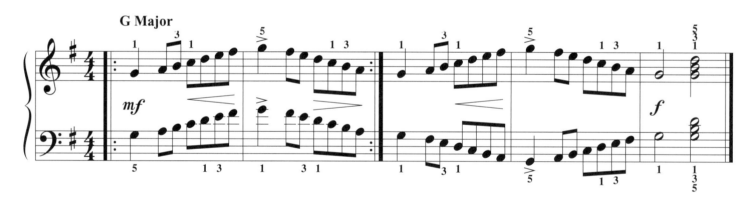

G Major

Andante ♩ = 69 ___   *Moderato* ♩ = 80 ___   *Allegro* ♩ = 92 ___

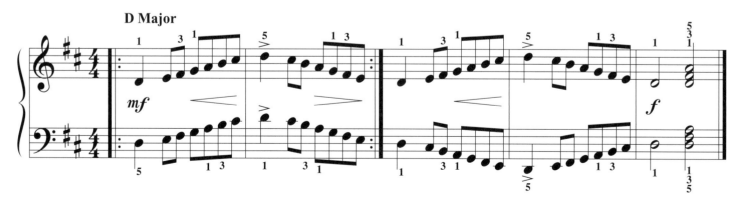

D Major

Andante ♩ = 69 ___   *Moderato* ♩ = 80 ___   *Allegro* ♩ = 92 ___

F Major

Andante ♩ = 69 ___   *Moderato* ♩ = 80 ___   *Allegro* ♩ = 92 ___

A Harmonic Minor

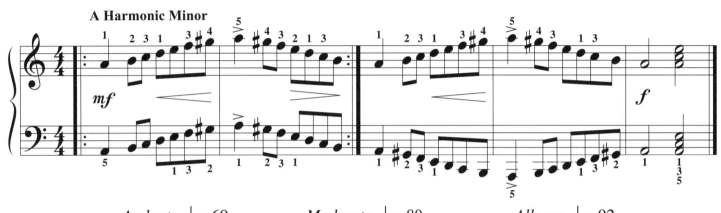

Andante ♩ = 69 ___   *Moderato* ♩ = 80 ___   *Allegro* ♩ = 92 ___

D Harmonic Minor

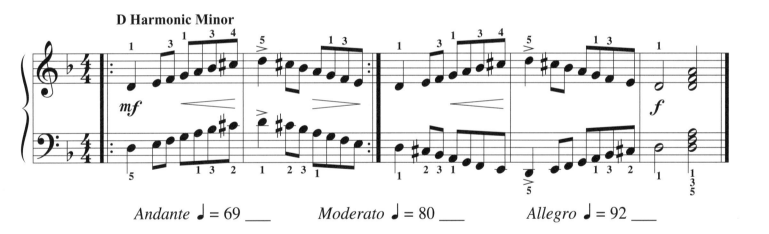

Andante ♩ = 69 ___   *Moderato* ♩ = 80 ___   *Allegro* ♩ = 92 ___

E Harmonic Minor

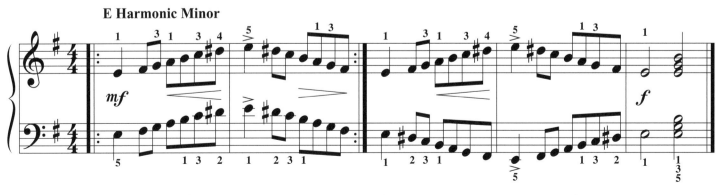

Andante ♩ = 69 ___   *Moderato* ♩ = 80 ___   *Allegro* ♩ = 92 ___

Chord Chart

Primary Chords in Major Keys

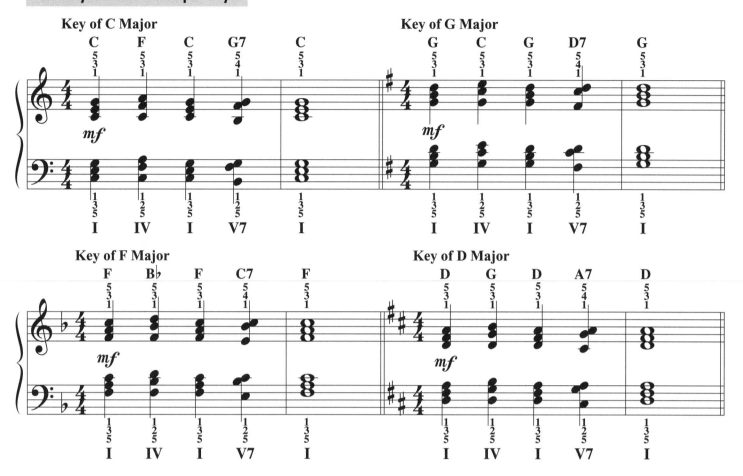

Primary Chords in Minor Keys

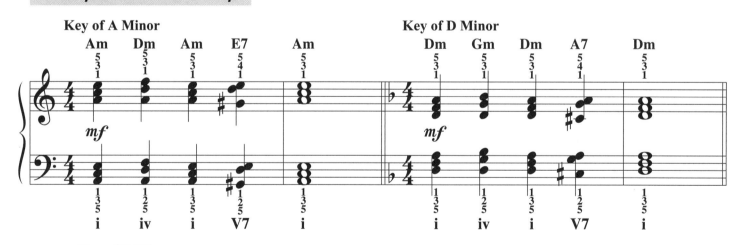

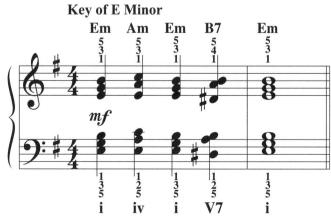

The 12 Major Triads

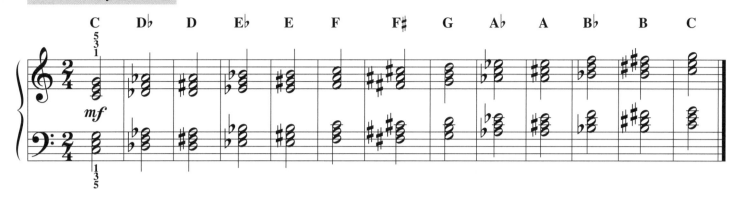

The 12 Minor Triads

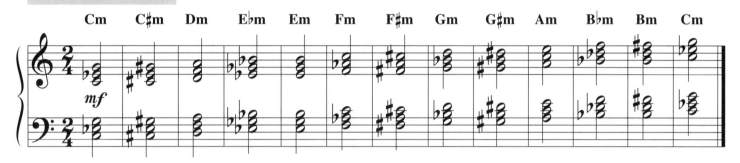

Triad Inversions

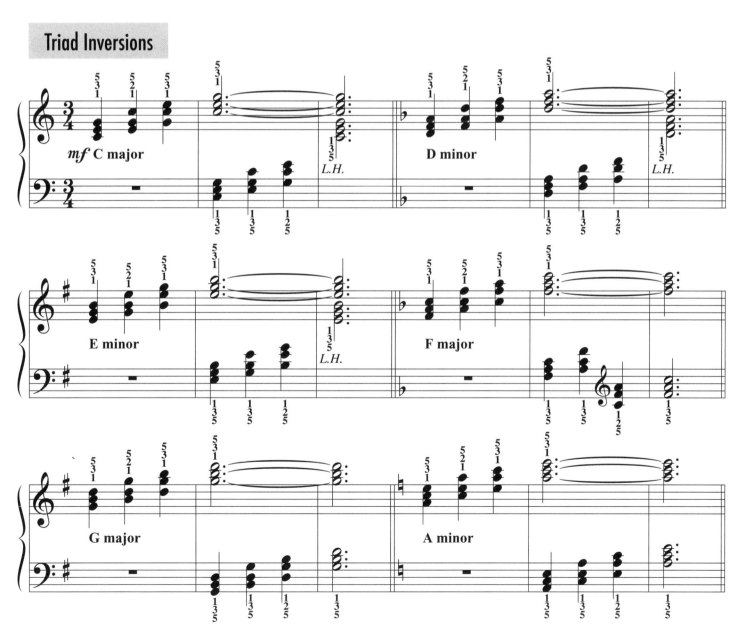

195

Dictionary

DYNAMIC MARKS

pp	**p**	**mp**	**mf**	**f**	**ff**
pianissimo	*piano*	*mezzo piano*	*mezzo forte*	*forte*	*fortissimo*
very soft	soft	moderately soft	moderately loud	loud	very loud

crescendo (cresc.)
Play gradually louder.

diminuendo (dim.) or decrescendo (decresc.)
Play gradually softer.

SIGN	TERM	DEFINITION
	a tempo	Returning to the beginning tempo (speed). (See p. 19)
	accent mark	Play this note louder.
	accidental	Sharps, flats, or naturals added to a piece and not in the key signature.
	accompaniment	The harmony and rhythm that accompany the melody. (See p. 29)
	Alberti bass	A left-hand accompaniment that outlines the notes of a chord using the pattern: bottom-top-middle-top. (See pp. 68, 70, 90)
	Allegretto	Cheerful; rather fast. (See p. 78)
	Allegro	Fast, lively tempo. (See p. 36)
	Allegro moderato	Moderately fast. (See p. 14)
	Andante	Walking tempo. (See p. 22)
	arpeggio	"Harp-like." The notes of a chord played one after another, going up or down. (See pp. 18, 47, 83, 153, 169, 174, 175, 177)
	binary form (AB)	A musical form with two sections (section A and section B). Each section usually repeats. (See pp. 14, 57)
	blocked chord	The tones of a chord or interval played together. (See p. 28)
	broken chord	The tones of a chord or interval played separately. (See p. 29)
	chord	Three or more tones sounding together. (See p. 12)
	chord analysis	Naming the chord letter names (Ex. Dm) or the Roman numerals (Ex. I, IV, V7) of a piece. (See pp. 48, 49)
	chord symbol	The letter name of a chord indicated above the music. A lowercase "m" is used to show minor. (See pp. 48, 49)

	chorus	A repeated section (music and lyrics) of a popular piece that often features the words of the title. (See p. 162)
	close position	The closest position of chord tones; avoiding leaps between chords. (See pp. 12, 13)
	coda	Ending section. (See p. 19)
	common time	$\frac{4}{4}$ time. (See p. 103)
	contrary motion	Two musical lines moving in opposite directions at the same time. (See p. 157)
¢	**cut time** *(alla breve)*	Short for $\frac{2}{2}$ time. The half note receives the beat (Two half-note beats per measure). (See p. 104)
D.C. al Coda	***Da Capo al Coda***	Return to the beginning and play to ⊕, then jump to the *Coda*. (See pp. 19, 25)
D.C. al Fine	***Da Capo al Fine***	Return to the beginning and play until *Fine* (end). (See p. 37)
	damper pedal	The right pedal, which sustains the sound, played with the right foot. (See pp. 9, 20)
	dominant	Scale degree 5 or the chord built on scale degree 5. (See p. 34)
	dominant 7th chord	A four-note chord built in 3rds on scale degree 5 (the dominant). (See p. 35)
	dotted quarter note	A dot adds half the value to the note. A dotted quarter is the equivalent of a quarter note tied to an eighth note. (See p. 74)
⅞	**eighth rest**	Silence for the value of an eighth note. (See p. 64)
	etude	A piece of music for the development of a certain technical skill. (See p. 40)
⌢	*fermata*	Hold this note longer than its normal value. (See p. 19)
1. 2.	**1st and 2nd endings**	Play the 1st ending and repeat. Then play the 2nd ending, skipping over the 1st ending. (See p. 15)
	gavotte	A lively French dance in $\frac{4}{4}$ time. It usually begins with two upbeats. (See p. 57)
	half step	The distance from one key to the very closest key on the keyboard. (Ex. C-C♯, or E-F) (See p. 12)
	harmonic minor scale	The form of the minor scale that has a raised 7th scale degree. An accidental is used to raise the 7th note a half step. (See pp. 87, 111, 145)

SIGN	TERM	DEFINITION
	harmony	Notes or chords played along with the melody.
	imitation	The immediate repetition of a musical idea played by the other hand. (See p. 36)
	interval	The distance between two musical tones, keys on the keyboard, or notes on the staff. (Ex. 2nd, 3rd, 4th, 5th) (See pp. 10, 11, 16, 102)
	inversion	Rearranging the notes of a chord. Ex. C-E-G may invert to E-G-C or G-C-E. (See pp. 54, 56)
	key signature	The key signature appears at the beginning of each line of music. It indicates sharps or flats to be used throughout the piece. (See p. 30)
	lead sheet	The melody only, with chord symbols written above the staff. (See p. 28)
	leading tone	Scale degree 7. (See p. 30)
	ledger lines	Short lines used to extend the staff. (See pp. 16, 22, 94, 134)
	legato	Smooth, connected. (See p. 18)
	major scale	An eight-note scale with half steps between scale degrees 3–4 and 7–8. (See pp. 12, 13, 30, 156)
	minor scale	An eight-note scale with half steps between scale degrees 2–3 and 5–6. (See pp. 86–87, 110–111, 144–145)
	Moderato	Moderate tempo (See p. 24)
	molto	Much, very. (See p. 181)
	motive	A short musical idea. (See p. 36)
	natural	A natural (always a white key) cancels a sharp or a flat. (See p. 25)
	natural minor scale	The form of the minor scale that uses only the notes of the key signature. (See pp. 87, 111, 145)
	nocturne	Night piece. (See p. 186)
	octave	The interval that spans eight letter names. (Ex. C to C) (See pp. 142, 160, 174)
	opera	A drama set to music, with singing, acting, and sometimes dancing. (See pp. 114, 132, 182)

	ostinato	A musical pattern that is repeated over and over. (See p. 88)
8*va* – ⌐	*ottava*	Play one octave higher (or lower) than written. (See p. 19)
	parallel motion	Two musical lines moving in the same direction at the same time. (See p. 157)
——∧——	**pedal mark**	Shows the down-up motion of the damper pedal. (See p. 20)
ped. simile	*pedale simile*	Pedal similarly. (See p. 29)
⌣	**phrase**	A musical sentence. A phrase is often shown by a slur, also called a phrase mark. (See p. 32)
	poco	A little.
I, IV, V	**primary chords**	The I, IV, and V chords are the primary chords in a major key. The i, iv, and V chords are the primary chords in a minor key. (See pp. 12, 13, 92, 112, 146, 158)
	relative minor	The minor key that shares the same key signature as its relative major. The relative minor is three half steps below the tonic of the major key. (See pp. 88, 90)
‖: :‖	**repeat signs**	Play the music within the repeat signs again. (See pp. 14–15)
rit.	*ritardando*	Gradually slowing down. (See p. 15)
	root	The chord tone that is the letter name of the chord. (See p. 12)
𝄢	**root position**	The letter name of the chord is the lowest note. (See p. 12)
	rotation	A back-and-forth rocking motion of the hand. (See pp. 41, 60)
	scale degree	The numeric position of the tone in the scale. (See p. 12)
	secondary chords	Chords built on scale degrees 2, 3, 6, and 7. (See p. 48)
𝄢	**seventh (7th)**	The interval of a 7th spans seven letter names. (Ex. A–G) On the staff, a 7th is a from line to a line or a space to a space. (See p. 102)
sfz	*sforzando*	A sudden, strong accent. (See p. 116)
	sightread	Playing through a piece for the first time (at sight).
♫♫	**sixteenth notes**	Four sixteenth notes equal one quarter note. (See p. 178)
♪♪♪	**slur**	A curved line that indicates legato playing.

SIGN	TERM	DEFINITION
♩̣	**staccato**	Detached, disconnected.
	string quartet	A string ensemble comprised of two violins, viola, and cello. (See p. 186)
sub.	*subito*	Suddenly. (See p. 106)
	suite	A set of short pieces, often written in dance forms. (See p. 138)
sus4	**suspended-4 chord**	A three-note chord that uses the 4th instead of the 3rd. (See pp. 27, 122)
	swing rhythm	Eighth notes played in a long-short pattern. (♫ = ♩♪) (See p. 38)
	symphony	A long composition for orchestra usually consisting of three or four related movements. (See pp. 96, 160)
𝄢 ♪. ♪	**syncopation**	A shift of accent to the weaker beats, or between the beats. (See pp. 66, 172)
	tempo	The speed of the music.
♩̠	**tenuto mark**	Hold this note its full value. Press gently into the key. (See p. 148)
𝄢 oooooooo	**tonic**	Scale degree 1. (The tone on which a scale is built.) Also, a triad built on the tonic note. (See pp. 30, 86, 110, 144, 156)
𝄢 ♯𝄞	**triad**	A 3-note chord built in 3rds. (See p. 48)
♫♫	**triplet**	Three eighth notes to a quarter note. (See p. 96)
	upbeat (pick-up note)	The note(s) of an incomplete opening measure. (See pp. 21, 28)
	variation	An alteration of the theme: different notes, rhythm, dynamics, etc. (See p. 118)
	verse	A section of a song that changes lyrics with each repeat. A verse(s) leads into the chorus. (See p. 162)
	waltz	A dance piece in ¾ time. (See pp. 109, 119)
	whole step	The distance of two half steps. (See p. 12)